HOW WE GOT OUR BIBLE

AND

WHY WE BELIEVE
IT IS GOD'S WORD

HOW WE GOT OUR BIBLE

AND

WHY WE BELIEVE IT IS GOD'S WORD

By
W. H. GRIFFITH THOMAS

MOODY PRESS
CHICAGO

Copyright, 1926, by
The Moody Bible Institute
of Chicago

ISBN: 0-8024-3976-6

Printed in the United States of America

CONTENTS

CHAPTER	PAGE
Foreword	7
1. Structure and History of the Bible	9
2. Canonicity of the Bible	19
3. Authority of the Bible	27
4. Authority of the Bible—Continued	35
5. Trustworthiness of the Old Testament	47
6. Trustworthiness of the New Testament	55
7. Unity of the Bible	65
8. Progressiveness of the Bible	75
9. Inspiration of the Bible	85
10. Inspiration of the Bible—Continued	95
11. Interpretation of the Bible	105
12. Purpose of the Bible	115

FOREWORD

APPEARING as a posthumous work of that dean of Bible teachers, Dr. W. H. Griffith Thomas, this volume should have a special appeal to all who knew and loved the author, or who are familiar with his earlier works. The Rev. W. Graham Scroggie has said that "the reading of Dr. Thomas' books creates in one a deeper love of and desire for God as revealed in his Word," and this is strikingly true of this clear and satisfying marshaling of evidence as to what the Bible is. These studies have appeared serially in the Friends' Witness under the title, "The Book of Books." In order that the book may be more readily available for class or individual study, a series of questions, prepared by the Rev. Robert M. Webster, of the Philadelphia School of the Bible, and the Pennsylvania Bible Institute,

Philadelphia, have been added at the end of each chapter.

Dr. Thomas was born in England in 1861. Minister, scholar, teacher, and author, he held important posts such as Fellow of King's College, London; principalship of Wycliffe Hall, Oxford; and professorship at Wycliffe College, Toronto. He was a regular Keswick speaker and cofounder of Dallas Theological Seminary. His writings include commentaries, theologies, devotionals, and outstanding biographies on the apostles Peter and John. He died in 1924.

1

STRUCTURE AND HISTORY OF THE BIBLE

OUR ENGLISH VERSION, and probably most of the translations of the Bible, consists of sixty-six Books, thirty-nine in the Old Testament and twenty-seven in the New, and is regarded with special consideration by all Christians because it is held to be the record of the divine religion of Redemption.

The Old Testament shows how this religion was prepared through many centuries; the New tells how it was at length provided and proclaimed. The keynote of the former is, therefore, Preparation, and this is twofold: the preparation of the Redeemer for the people; and the preparation of the people for the Redeemer. The keynote of the latter is Manifestation, and this is also twofold: the manifestation of the Redeemer in Person, and the consequent manifestation of his grace in the redeemed, both individually in believers and corporately in the community of Christians, which we call the church. Thus both Testaments together form a complete record of human sin and divine salvation, the former making the latter necessary. Sin is seen in its nature and consequences, and salvation in its character and effects.

The Books of the Old Testament are the product of at least thirty authors and cover a period of at least a thousand years. They are made up of history, legislation, poetry, philosophy and prophecy. The Jewish Old Testament, following the classification of the Hebrew text, is in three parts; the law, the prophets, and the psalms. The law consists of the first five books of the Bible and on this account is called the Pentateuch (five rolls). It may be said in passing that there is no trace in the historical tradition of the Jews of a Hexateuch (six rolls, including Joshua). The second division of the Hebrew Bible, called the prophets, includes the historical books of Judges, Samuel and Kings, and the prophetic books proper with the exception of Daniel, which because it is apocalyptic rather than, as the other prophetic books, strictly predictive, is in the third section. The historical books are called "the former prophets" because they are written from a religious standpoint and are not mere historical annals. They were pretty certainly the work of prophets or prophetic men. The third part of the Hebrew Bible is so called from the first book in it, and the rest of it consists of those Books which are not found in the other two parts. Our English Old Testament has a different order and comes from the Greek Version of the Old Testament. It consists of four parts: Pentateuch, History, Poetry, and Prophecy.

The New Testament numbers twenty-seven Books, and is the work of eight authors, covering only about fifty years. Of the eight authors, five were apostles of Christ and three were associates of the apostles. The New Testament has three main parts: History, contained in the Gospels and Acts; Doctrine, in the Epistles; and Prophecy, in the Revelation. These three provide respectively the commencement, the course, and the culmination of the Christian religion.

There is a striking connection between the Old Testament and the New beyond the general unity mentioned above. The Old Testament emphasizes the three aspects of the divine Saviour: the prophet, the priest, and the king. These answer to the three deepest necessities of man. He requires a prophet to reveal God; a priest to redeem from sin; and a king to rule his life for God. Each of these is emphasized in the Old Testament, and in general can be associated with sections of its Books. The New Testament fitly shows how this threefold need is met in Christ as Prophet, Priest, and King; revealing, redeeming, and ruling. The full title "Jesus Christ our Lord" suggests this: Jesus the Prophet, Christ the Priest, and the Lord the King.

Such is the Bible as we have it today. But how did it come to be what it now is? There has been a gradual growth, and the steps of this we must note. At first and for a long time the revelation of God was oral. "The word of the Lord came to Abram" (Gen. 15:1). This was sufficient for ages. But the time came when it was necessary to put the divine revelation in a written form. It would seem as though a book were essential for the maintenance and continuance of religion, and it is at least interesting and perhaps also significant that all the great religious systems of the world have their sacred books. Literature is the nearest possible approach to reliability. This is a point which will need fuller consideration at a later stage.

There are traces in the Old Testament of a gradual growth by accretion. The Jewish tradition associates Moses with the commencement

STRUCTURE AND HISTORY OF THE BIBLE 13

of the Scripture, and there is no doubt of the essential truth of this position. Certainly there is no other tradition attaching to the books; and in view of the tenacity with which the Jews kept their national traditions, this belief about Moses calls for adequate explanation. A careful study of passages found throughout the Old Testament shows this development, indications being found at almost every period, of growth and additions to the existing writings. Among others the following passages should be noted: Exodus 17:14; Numbers 33:2; Deuteronomy 17:18; Joshua 1:8; 24:26; 1 Samuel 10:25; Isaiah 8:16, 20; Jeremiah 36:2; Daniel 9:2; Nehemiah 8:1. These references, taken from each period of the history, indicate a gradual growth of the Jewish Scriptures. The complete volume is associated by tradition with Ezra, and there are no valid reasons for doubting this, especially as it harmonizes with the testimony of the well-informed and representative Jew, Josephus, who, writing in the first century of the Christian Era, said that no book was added to the Jewish Scripture after the time of Malachi. As to the preservation of the gradually growing volume through the ages from Moses to Ezra, it has been pointed out by that eminent Egyptologist, Professor Naville, that it was the custom among Eastern nations to deposit their books in their sanctuaries, and there is every likelihood that the Jews did the same. The copy found by Hilkiah was probably this temple copy (2 Kings 22:8).

The New Testament was also marked by a gradual growth. At first came the oral accounts of the life of Christ and the presentation of the Christian message. Then followed the apostolic letters, confirming and elaborating their oral teaching. These letters were read in the assemblies of the Christians (1 Thess. 5:27; 2 Thess. 3:14). The next stage was the interchange of these letters among the churches (Col. 4:16). Not long after the need of a record of the life of the founder was felt, and as a result came our Gospels (Luke 1:1-4; John 20:31). The story of the early church naturally followed (Acts), and the Apocalypse fitly crowned the whole with its outlook on the future. As the primitive churches had the Old Testament volume in their hands, it was a constant reminder of the need of an analogous volume of the New Testament, though everything was so very gradual and natural that it is only when the process is complete that it is realized to have been also manifestly supernatural.

At this point the important question arises how we can be sure that our Bible today really represents the books which have been thus naturally and simply collected into a volume.

Structure and History of the Bible 15

The answer is that it is quite easy to prove that our Bible is the same as the church has had through the centuries. We start with the printed Bibles of today and it is obviously easy to show that they correspond with the printed Bibles of the sixteenth century, or the time when printing was invented. From these we can go back through the English and Latin versions until we reach to the great manuscripts of the fourth century as represented by the three outstanding codices known as the Codex Sinaiticus (in Petrograd), the Codex Vaticanus (in Rome) and the Codex Alexandrinus (in the British Museum). Then we can go back still farther and compare the use of Scripture in the writings of the Fathers of the third century, and from these work back to the second century when versions in several languages are found. From this it is but a short step to the time of the apostles and the actual composition of the New Testament writings. There is no reasonable doubt that we possess today what has always been regarded as the Scriptures of the Christian Church.

The proof as to the Old Testament can be shown along similar lines. Our Old Testament is identical with the Bible of the Jews at the present time. This is the translation of Hebrew manuscripts dating from several centuries past, and the fact of the Jews always having used the same

Bible as they do today is a proof that all through the ages the Christian Church has not been mistaken in its inclusion of the Old Testament in its Bible. An additional evidence of great value is the fact that the Hebrew Bible was translated into Greek about two centuries before Christ, and this translation is essentially the same as the Hebrew text from which we get our Old Testament. The additional books which are found in the Greek Old Testament, called the Apocrypha, were never part of the Jewish Scriptures, and were never regarded as Scripture by those who knew the Hebrew language. These books were not written in Hebrew, and were not included in Scripture by any body of Christians until the Church of Rome arbitrarily decided to include them at the Council of Trent in the sixteenth century. In addition to other points which could be mentioned, these books contain inaccuracies in history and doctrine, which make it impossible for them to be regarded as part of the Word of God for man.

These are some of the facts which are connected with our Bible as we now have it, and from them we can proceed to consider the various points which are involved in our belief that the Bible is for us the Word of God, and as such, the rule of our faith and practice.

STRUCTURE AND HISTORY OF THE BIBLE 17

QUESTIONS

1. Into how many Books is the Bible divided? How many in the Old Testament? How many in the New Testament?
2. Why is the Bible regarded with special consideration by all Christians? What is the keynote of the Old Testament? What is the keynote of the New Testament?
3. How many Old Testament writers were there? How long a period was covered in the writing of the Old Testament?
4. How many New Testament writers were there? How long a period was covered in the writing of the New Testament?
5. What arrangement of Books was followed in the Hebrew Old Testament? In what New Testament passage is this arrangement referred to? What is the New Testament arrangement of the Books? What do these sections respectively provide?
6. What aspects of Christ, essential to man's need, are specially emphasized in the Old Testament? How does the New Testament show that this need is met? How does our Lord's full title suggest this?
7. What does the Old Testament show concerning the method of its formation? Whom does Jewish tradition associate with its beginning? Whom does it associate with its completion? What explanation has been offered to account for the preservation of the volume?
8. What was the method of the formation of the New Testament? State the probable general order of the appearance of the several groups of Books.
9. Can we be sure that our Bible of today really represents the Books originally collected into one volume? How may this be shown as to the Old Testament? How may this be shown as to the New Testament?
10. What is the Apocrypha? Was it included in the canon of the Hebrew Old Testament? By what authority does it appear in certain modern editions of the Bible?

2

CANONICITY OF THE BIBLE

THE ATTITUDE of the Christian Church toward the entire volume of the Scriptures is one of reverence. The thirty-nine Books of the Old Testament comprise the Bible of the Jews, setting forth the Jewish religion in its historical development and different aspects, covering centuries of time. The Church, therefore, inherited her belief in the sacredness and authority of the Old Testament, from our Lord and his apostles, since the basis of their teaching was the Old Testament Scriptures. Since the New Testament sets forth the Christian religion in various aspects, covering some sixty years, or two generations, and is thus a complete declaration of those facts on which the Church grounds her life and belief, her reverence for it is readily understood. None of the Books of the New Testament was written by the Founder of the Christian religion, in marked contrast with the Koran, which is alleged to have been written by Mohammed. From the beginning of her life the Church had the Old Testament, but not until years had passed were the Books constituting the New Testament written, and added to it. The recognition of these New Testament writings as possessed of divine authority, marked them as canonical, and the method by which they were so recognized has been called canonization.

The word "Canon" comes from the Greek word, *Kanon*, and is akin to the Hebrew word for reed. The words "cane" and "canon" are cognate terms. The word had active and passive senses. A thing which is employed as a measure is first measured, and only then used to measure other things. The passive meaning, anything measured, e.g., a measured racecourse at Olympia in turn becomes a measure, and the word means a straight rod or rule used for measurement (2 Cor. 10: 13-16, passive; Gal. 6: 16, active). Then the word came to mean any list of things for reference, e.g., at Alexandria a list of classical writers was called a "Canon," and Eusebius calls chronological tables, "Canons of times."

This is the meaning of the technical word

CANONICITY OF THE BIBLE

"Canon" in relation to Scripture. The Canon of Scripture is used first of all in a *passive* sense, meaning that which being measured becomes the means which measures or tests others. Thus Scripture is (1) that which is measured or defined by the rule of the Christian Church, and (2) that which, being measured, becomes thereby the rule of the Church for other cases. The Bible contains the recognized list of Books which have been measured by a certain rule or standard of measurement and have thereby become measures of other books. The word is first used in the Christian Church by a poet, Amphilochius, 380, "The Canon of the God-breathed writings." But Origen had spoken of "canonized books" or books put on the list. Afterward Jerome and Augustine, A.D. 400, handled the word technically.

What, then, is the rule of the Christian Church by which a book is "measured," or defined as "canonical"? The Sixth Article of the Church of England describes a Canonical Book as one "of whose authority [there] was never any doubt in the Church." We must observe that the reference is to authority, not to authorship. The statement is usually regarded as a great difficulty, since it cannot apply to all the books and all the churches, for the Reformers knew well the early doubts about some of the books. It is probable that as the doubts were dead by the sixteenth century the reference is to the Church as a whole as distinct from individual churches. The matter was originally settled mainly by public reading and general usage in Christian communities. The first three centuries never pronounced on the subject except by the testimony of individual and representative writers. No corporate evidence was possible. But when that was available and necessary it was soon seen that there was no real doubt as to our books. The first corporate witness dates from the Council of Laodicea, A.D. 364, where the testimony is clear, and when once the whole Church was able to bear its witness the words of the Article are seen to be justified.

The grounds of Canonicity need consideration. Why were certain books received and certain rejected? In conversation with a friend I asked him this question: "What is the ultimate reason why you accept the New Testament? Deep down below everything else, what is it that causes you to accept it, and reject other books?" My friend said he did not know that he had ever really faced it in that way. So I went on: "Do you accept it because it is old? There are older books. Do you accept it because it contains truth? Well, there are other books that contain truth. No: beneath its age, beneath its helpfulness, beneath its truthfulness is the bedrock — this book came from men who were uniquely qualified to convey God's will to men; and the basis of our accep-

CANONICITY OF THE BIBLE 23

tance of the New Testament is what is called in technical language 'Apostolicity'; because the books came either from Apostolic authors, or through Apostolic sanction." Our view of the Old Testament corresponds to this.

The fundamental reason is the conviction that certain books came from men who were divinely inspired to reveal and convey God's will; prophets in the Old Testament and apostles in the New. Prophets were recognized expounders of God's will, and their writings were regarded as immediately authoritative. The best illustration is found in Jeremiah 36, where the prophet's words were recognized as possessing authority at once. Each book had this authority by reason of its prophetic source, and then gradually came the collection into one volume, so that the Old Testament represents those books which Israel accepted on proper evidence as the divine standard of faith and practice, because they were either written or put forth by prophetic men. It was not the decision of the people that caused the Canonicity, but the Canonicity was the cause of their acceptance by the people. The authority came from God through the prophets, and the recognition by the people was the effect of the Canonicity. The action of the people was the weighing of evidence, and the outcome was testimony rather than judgment.

In the same way the books of the New Testament were regarded as marked by Apostolic origin. This may have been authorship or sanction, but there is no doubt that the primary standard of verification and acceptance was the belief that these books came from Apostolic men, either apostles themselves or their associates. So that the ground of Canonicity was not merely the age, or the truth, or the helpfulness of the books, but, beneath and before these characteristics, because they came from uniquely qualified instruments of God's will. All other tests were subsidiary and confirmatory. It is, therefore, important and essential to distinguish between the *ground* of Canonicity and the ground of the *conviction* of Canonicity. The latter is quite separate from the former and is subjective, while the latter is rational, objective, and leaves man no excuse.

It is particularly important at this point, to notice what Canonicity really implies and involves. It created a book, not a revelation. Canonicity is analogous to codification, and implies the existence of separate books. The authority of each book of the Bible would have been the same even if there had been no collection and codification. So that the authority is not that of a volume, but of a revelation; the revelation did not come to exist because of the Canonicity but the Canonicity because of the revelation, and the

CANONICITY OF THE BIBLE

Bible, as we have seen, is regarded as a revelation, because it is held to be the embodiment of the historical manifestation of the Redeemer and his truth. It has been well said that *the Bible is not an authorized collection of books, but a collection of authorized books.* This distinction is vital. It is essential to remember that the quality which determines acceptance of a book is its possession of a divine revelation. So that Canonicity did not raise a book to the position of Scripture, but recognized that it was already Scripture. Canonization was a decision based on testimony, and the canonizing process was the recognition of an existing fact. It is, of course, true that the process of canonization by the whole Church implies a cumulative authority, and adds immensely to the strength of the position as representing the witness of the entire Christian body, but it must never be forgotten that the authority of each separate book was in it from the first.

QUESTIONS

1. What has ever been the attitude of the Christian Church toward the Scriptures?
2. What two words describe the fact of the recognition of the divine authority of the Scriptures, and the method by which they were so recognized? What is the origin and the meaning of these words?

3. How did the Books of the New Testament become canonical? When was the first corporate testimony to canonicity given?
4. What are the grounds of the canonicity of the Old Testament Books?
5. What are the grounds of the canonicity of the New Testament Books?
6. What does canonicity involve? To what is it analogous?
7. What effect would a failure to canonize the different Books of the Bible have had on their authority?
8. Did the revelation of truth come to be because of canonicity? State the facts of the case.
9. What has the Bible sometimes been said to be?
10. What was canonization? What was the canonizing process?

3

AUTHORITY OF THE BIBLE

THE ACCEPTANCE of the Bible is due to the belief that it embodies a divine Revelation. Religion involves a Revelation, but it is necessary to inquire as to the grounds on which the Bible is regarded as containing and expressing that Revelation.

No one can read the Old or the New Testament without seeing indications that the writers believed that they could and did receive communications from God (Gen. 15:1; Ezek. 6:1; Luke 3:2; 1 Thess. 4:15).

At this point some fundamental presuppositions must be considered. First, Revelation is possible. If we believe that God exists and is almighty, then of course he can communicate himself to us. Second, Revelation is probable, inasmuch as self-revelation is natural to us. We cannot help communicating ourselves to others, because of interest and love, and, as God is love, this fact implies that he will communicate himself, because it is the essence of love to reveal itself. Third, Revelation is necessary. There are two things essential for life — Knowledge and Power; what Matthew Arnold once called "light and leading." And these are all the more needed because of sin. Sin has brought uncertainty, and this demands knowledge. Sin has brought weakness, and this necessitates power.

These considerations lead to the thought that Revelation is available in the Person of the Lord Jesus Christ (Heb. 1:1, 2). A person communicates himself by acts or by words, or by both. For the first disciples, for the earliest Christian Church before our Lord's resurrection—that is to say, for the community of his immediate followers — his Presence was a revelation, his Person was sufficient; but we today have his words, since we have not his outward Presence as they had (John 20:30, 31; 2 Tim. 3:16, 17).

Our position therefore is this — God has revealed himself in nature, in providence and in history; but preëminently he has revealed himself in Christ for spiritual realities. Natural religion has not been found sufficient for human life, because of sin. Man's nature has never been an adequate mirror of divine revelation.

Now of this revelation in Christ, we believe that the New Testament is the purest, fullest, and clearest expression and embodiment. We are not concerned for the moment whether the revelation came in this way or in that way. All that is essential is that we have — whatever it is and however it has come — a revelation of God in Christ. It is at least significant to note that all the great religions have their sacred books. It would seem as though the *litera scripta* (the written word) were a foundation, a necessary condition of all divine revelation.

We proceed to state that Revelation is assured. This is the heart of our present subject: Why do we believe the Bible to be a divine revelation? I do not now refer to the Old Testament in detail, because if we can prove the New Testament to be divine this carries the Old Testament with it. We are on the most convenient ground if we concentrate on the New Testament, and look upon that as the embodiment of a divine revelation. There are just three steps in this argument.

First, the New Testament is genuine; that is, it is the work of those for whom it is claimed—the early believers in Jesus Christ. This genuineness of the New Testament may be proved in a variety of ways. (a) There is the testimony of the Church through the centuries. (b) There is the direct testimony of the Books themselves. If we examine them we see clear evidence that they came from the apostles' time. It is easy to see the New Testament possesses evidences of genuineness. Its allusions to Jewish, Roman, and Greek history and customs prove its early date. Such allusions would have been impossible later. (c) There is the testimony of adversaries. Every opposition to Christianity from the second century onward has been directed toward the New Testament. Why did men like Celsus, Porphyry, Julian, and Rousseau oppose it? If they did not think anything of this book, why did they trouble about it?

Secondly, the New Testament is credible; that is, it is worthy to be believed. There are many books genuine, but not credible. The New Testament is not only genuine, but is worthy of our belief. Why? For several reasons. Because of the unblemished character of the witnesses. Because of the agreement of the facts of the New Testament with the acts of Christianity in the world. Because the contents of the New Testament do nothing but good. Because the explorations of Palestine, Egypt, and Babylon go to confirm the truth of the Bible, Old and New Testaments. There have been many archeological researches, and not one has gone against the Bible, or proved it untrue.

AUTHORITY OF THE BIBLE 31

Now, if we have followed the argument so far, we shall be prepared to take the third step. The New Testament is divine. What are the reasons for this? There are many ways of proving it, some of which will come before us later. But now attention is concentrated on three points, which will be sufficient for the purpose.

First, there is that in the Old Testament which is always pointing forward to the future, especially to the coming of the Messiah. In Liddon's Bampton Lectures it is shown that there are 333 references to the Messiah in the Old Testament, and Dr. Pierson argued that, based upon mathematical grounds, the concentration of all these 333 references on an individual, in face of all probabilities against it, is nothing short of marvelous. Each time we add a reference, we reduce the probability of the allusions centering on one person; and when we get to 333, and all these concentrate on one Man, we see at once the force of this extraordinary expectation. And what does the power of prediction mean but the Supernatural?

Then, we turn to the New Testament and consider the Person of our Lord Jesus Christ. We notice the portrait of Christ, and note the combination and balance of qualities in him, and the perfection of his character.

The third of these proofs or attestations concerns the results of Christianity. Let us observe the effects of Christianity on life. Life is the problem, and Christ is the solution; life is the question, and Christ is the answer. If we want to see the results of Christianity, we should test it by other religions. If we would know what Confucianism has done, let us look at China; if we would know what Buddhism has done, let us look at India; if we would know what Islam has done, let us look at Turkey and Persia. We do not despise any of these religions. Everything that is good in them comes from God. They are what Tennyson calls "broken lights." But while they are "lights," they are "broken." There is one great difference between them and Christianity; in each of these, man is seeking God; in Christianity. God is seeking man. These religions are human aspirations; Christianity is a divine revelation.

And so, we conclude that God has spoken; and this message is in the Bible or nowhere else. It calls for a personal test from every one of us. In the present day a great deal is rightly said about the argument from experience. There is no other book in the world that will so verify itself to human experience, and this is because it contains and embodies a divine revelation. Whatever may be said about history and philosophy and morality, the crowning point is: What is the

AUTHORITY OF THE BIBLE

Bible to us? And when the Bible is really a force in our own heart and life, we cannot possibly doubt that it comes from God.

QUESTIONS

1. What is the basis of the acceptance of the Bible?
2. State and define the three necessary presuppositions concerning revelation.
3. Who is the supreme revealer of God?
4. What is our position regarding revelation?
5. What is the clearest, fullest and most complete expression and embodiment of the revelation of God?
6. Why do we believe the Bible to be a divine revelation?
7. To what conclusion does all this lead?
8. What reasons may be assigned for this conclusion?
9. Compare, in a word, the ethnic religions and Christianity.
10. What one thing constitutes the Bible a unique book?

4

AUTHORITY OF THE BIBLE
(Continued)

IF GOD has spoken, then obviously his word must be authoritative. This question of authority is vital, and touches us at every point. A fundamental question is: What is the ultimate and final authority in religion? What and where is the last and supreme word concerning God, life, and eternity?

1. *The Need of Authority.* — Authority is needed in every walk of life, and it is also essential in connection with religion. Man, even as man, needs a guide. But still more, man as a sinner needs an authority.

2. *The Source of Authority.* — Where is this need to be satisfied? The answer, of course, is

that God is the Source of all authority, and authority is expressed by revelation. For the present purpose it will suffice to say that Christ, as representing and revealing God, is our ultimate authority. So far, there will be no real difficulty. But at once the question arises: God is invisible. Christ is no longer visibly here. Where, then, can this divine authority be found? Where is it embodied? And so we come to consider

3. *The Seat of Authority.* — There are three usual, perhaps only three possible answers. There are those who say that the seat of authority is in human reason. The word "reason" represents what is sometimes spoken of as human experience, including reason and conscience.

Some say that the consent of the mind is the condition and foundation of all certitude. Let us be clear on this point. Reason is valuable and necessary. "Thou shalt love the Lord thy God with all thy *mind*." The mind is essential as part of human nature, and is required to test the claims of any professed revelation, and then to receive the revelation thus tested. There can be no authority that destroys human reason; no authority that stultifies the mind that God has given us. The right of every man to verify is inalienable. "Prove all things," said the apostle, as well as "hold fast that which is good."

But this is very different from claiming that

AUTHORITY OF THE BIBLE 37

reason is the seat of authority. Man's faculties have been affected by sin. Besides, there is such a thing as reality, independent of reason. What is truth? Truth is not what I *trow*; truth is *fact*, and is not dependent upon the changing opinions of men. Truth is true whether we accept it or not. A thing must be true before we can accept it as truth. Truth is first objective — something presented — and only then is it subjective — something accepted. So that reason is not originative, not creative, it is only a channel. It is not a source, but a medium. It creates nothing; it only weighs data, and settles things as the result of weighing them.

Others say the *Church* is the seat of authority. On this, we ask: What Church? Where is that Church to be found? The Church in the fullest sense of the word is best described as "the blessed company of all faithful people"; and as such it is the product of divine revelation. The Church came into existence on the day of Pentecost by accepting divine revelation. As, therefore, the Church began through accepting divine revelation, it is difficult to see how it can be the seat of authority.

So we come to this, that the seat of authority is the *Bible*, and we believe this because the Bible preserves the revelation of Christ in its purest and clearest form. Christianity is a historic religion, and what we need today is the very best form of that historic religion which we can find. It does not matter where it is, or how it has come, so long as we can be sure that we possess the best available form of God's revelation in Christ.

Now Christianity is at once life and literature, and the life requires the literature for its nourishment. It is at least significant that all the great religions of the world have their books. It seems as though a book were really necessary for the maintenance and continuation of all religion. Literature is the nearest possible approach to reliability. Truth in literary form has four qualities which are preëminently necessary for a world-wide religion: (1) *Durability*. There is a character about a written form of communication which stands the test of time. (2) *Catholicity*. A universal element in a written form appeals and applies to the whole world. (3) *Fixity*. A permanence about the written Word makes it valuable and important for human life. (4) *Purity*. Purity is possible in connection with writing in a way that is impossible by any other method.

We cannot be sure of these four qualities in reason, because that is unsafe and variable. Nor can we be sure of them in any institution, for it is always uncertain. The written form of revelation is therefore the best available form.

If some one should say that this is what is called "Bibliolatry," the reply is that it is not. We do not interpose the Bible between ourselves and Christ. We use it as a medium by which we come to Christ. If I desire to see the stars with the telescope, will that be an interposition? It will be a medium. It will not be a hindrance, but a help. And so Scripture brings us face to face with the Lord Jesus Christ.

4. *The Nature of this Authority.* — It is a *spiritual* authority. It is a Book of salvation, it is a guide to spiritual safety. It reveals the Lord Jesus Christ as our Teacher, our Redeemer, and our Master; our Prophet, Priest, and King.

Then this authority is *supreme*. The Bible is supreme over reason. It is the light of reason and of human thought. Revelation, because it comes from God, cannot possibly dishonor reason, which also is from God. Reason is the judge of our need of revelation. It examines the claims of revelation; but once those claims are accepted, reason takes a subordinate place, and revelation is supreme. Reason examines, tests, sifts, inquires, but the moment it has become convinced that this or that comes from God, then, like Joshua of old, it says: "What saith my Lord unto his servant?" So, though revelation is supreme over reason, reason examines the credentials of revelation and then submits to them. Since

Christ is our Authority, what we need is the rational conviction that the Bible is the best form in which his Word reaches us, and then we submit to it, and it becomes supreme over our reason and life.

Again, the Bible is supreme over the Church. But some one says: "How can this be? Surely it is impossible; the Church was in existence at least twenty years before a line of the New Testament was written." The Church was certainly *before* the New Testament, but does it follow that the Church is *above* it? That is where a fallacy may creep in.

It is perfectly true that the Church had no part of the New Testament for more than twenty years, and there was no complete New Testament for a very long time after that. But while they did not possess the *written* Word they had the *spoken* Word from the day of Pentecost onward. The Church came into existence by believing the spoken Word; and as long as the apostles were at hand, the spoken Word was sufficient. But when they went from place to place, and afterward died, it was essential to embody the spoken revelation; and thus came the written form. It does not really matter whether it is spoken or written, so long as we can be sure it is a revelation from God. If the apostle Paul were present at our meetings we should listen to him just as carefully as we should read one of his writings. The precise way in which the revelation comes does not matter so long as we can be certain that it comes from God. So that it is perfectly true that the written Word of the New Testament came after the Church, but the spoken Word came before the Church.

Did the Church at Rome write the Epistle to the Romans? Was the Church at Rome the maker of that Epistle? No; it was the apostle who wrote that Epistle to the Church of Rome, and it was Scripture to that Church from the moment they accepted it from his hand. It was not the Church, but the apostles representing Christ, who gave first the spoken and then the written Word of God.

The Church is "a witness and a keeper" of Scripture, but it is not its *author* or *maker*, and the reasoning employed in support of the latter contention is fallacious. The fallacy, of course, lies in attributing to a body in its collective capacity certain acts of individual members of the body. The Church is not, and never was, the author of Scripture. The Scriptures are the law of God for the Church, delivered to it by the apostles and prophets.

So we say again that the Lord Jesus Christ is our supreme Authority, and we accept the Bible because it enshrines and embodies that authority. Take away Christ from the Bible, and there is no Bible left worth having. We do not bow down to the Book because it is a book; we do not repudiate reason because it is reason; we do not set aside the Church because it is the Church. We say that what we want is the best available form of Christ's revelation, and we believe we get this in the Bible and not in any other way.

The witness of the whole Church is very important, but still, when we have said everything for it, it is the work of a witness, not of a creator. As Bishop Gore has said: "The Word of God in the Bible is the final testing-ground of doctrine."

Church belief—what we call Church tradition — tends to deteriorate in the course of time. It never abides fixed. Tradition is so variable that we cannot depend upon it. There is modification and subtraction. We find this in Jewish history: "making the word of God of none effect through your tradition" (Mark 7:13). Bishop Gore wrote some years ago concerning the Jewish Church, and the Medieval Church, that they had "merged Scripture in a miscellaneous mass of authorities." We must not do this, but keep it separate and supreme.

The Bible is our final authority. The Old Testament could not claim finality for itself, because it was a gradual growth; and for the same reason

AUTHORITY OF THE BIBLE

the New Testament could not claim finality for itself; but the whole tone of the Bible involves and implies finality. The attitude of Scripture shows that it is final (Isa. 8:20; Matt. 24:25; 2 Cor. 4:2; Eph. 6:17; 1 Thess. 2:13; 2 Tim. 3:16; 1 Peter 1:23). Our Lord Jesus Christ himself in his life on earth bore testimony again and again to his own submission to that authority: "The Scripture cannot be broken" (See Matt. 5:18, and John 10:35). So we believe that the substance of Scripture bears testimony to its finality; and the general tenor of the early Church is in the same direction. If we read the Fathers of the first three centuries, we shall find witness after witness to the supremacy and finality of the Word of God, and at the Council of Chalcedon the Gospels were placed in the center, as the final court of appeal. Then, too, every heresy opposed to orthodoxy was alleged to be based on Scripture; ancient liturgies are simply saturated with the Scriptures, and the most severe attacks of opponents have always been on Scripture.

Experience tells the same story. It is clear from Church history that the Lord Jesus Christ has never fully revealed himself apart from the Bible. Where the Bible has been neglected, Christ has been neglected, and the light of Christianity has burned low. The oldest and truest view we have in ecclesiastical history is the supremacy of the Bible, and its finality in relation to the revelation of God in Christ.

There is a special reason today for asserting the authority of the Bible. In many quarters the emphasis is placed on experience and this is said to be the test of truth. Everything else is said to be objective and external, and if different from or opposed to experience, it is to be rejected. But experience is variable and uncertain, and cannot possibly be the criterion of truth. This modern tendency to fix the seat of authority within is liable to the fatal error of pure subjectivity, unless it is constantly safeguarded by the consciousness of a true objective element in knowledge. The idea of the terms "objective" and "external" being identical is wholly incorrect, for since the ultimate authority is Christ himself, we can see at once that though Christ is dwelling in us, he is not thereby identical with us. He is the divine revelation mediated through Scripture and applied by the Holy Spirit, and as such he is at once objective and subjective, external and internal. Years ago, Sabatier wrote a book entitled, "Religions of Authority and the Religion of the Spirit," a title which expresses an utterly false antithesis, because it is at least conceivable that a religion of the Spirit, in the sense of the Holy Spirit, can and will be a religion of "authority." Such a position is involved in a serious fallacy, because our supreme authority is the Lord Jesus Christ, and while he is not "external" he is certainly our final authority. It would be well if we could at once and forever get rid of the antithesis so often stated between objective and internal, because Christ as our authority is at once our indwelling Master and our absolutely objective authority.

Even the Christian consciousness is inadequate and often defective, because for a safe, reliable, and constant standard we need to look away from Christian experience, however true it may be. The truth underlying this emphasis on Christian experience can be stated without any disregard of Scripture as our standard. God's revelation in Christ is our supreme authority. Of this revelation the Bible is the divine authenticated record, and the Holy Spirit is the divinely authoritative interpreter, working on and in reason, conscience, and emotion, and producing an experience. It is thus that the truth without becomes the truth within and the subjective necessarily follows the objective. This makes our authority both external and internal and each fits the other. The Bible as an external authority alone would be without power in life. Our experience alone would be unsafe, unreliable, and independent of safeguards. But the two together are all we need. The Scripture tests experience and guards against the extremes of pure individualism, and the Spirit in our experience makes the truth of Scripture vital for life. Thus, the Scripture as interpreted by the Spirit protects us against the sole external authority of the Church and also against the sole internal authority of reason. The light of truth in the Bible blends with and guards the light of the Spirit within, and therein we have our ample, infallible and satisfying authority.

QUESTIONS

1. Is authority needed in religion? Why?
2. What is the source of authority? What question arises at this point?
3. What three answers to the question, "What is the seat of authority?" are possible? Explain each.
4. State four qualities which make a written revelation essential to religion. Explain each. What answer may be made to the charge of Bibliolatry?
5. What is the nature of this authority? What is the relation of reason to revelation? What is the relation of the Bible to the Church?
6. What is the relation of Christ to the Bible?
7. Did the Old Testament claim for itself finality? Why? Did the New Testament make such a claim? What is the attitude of the whole of Scripture to this claim?
8. What does Church History show concerning Christ's revelation of himself apart from the Scriptures?
9. What special need is there today for asserting the authority of the Bible?
10. Is Christian consciousness sufficient for a guide? What is our ample, infallible, and satisfying authority?

5

TRUSTWORTHINESS OF THE OLD TESTAMENT

It is apt to be overlooked that the fundamental question about the Bible is not its inspiration but its trustworthiness. It is possible to be without any theory of inspiration, if we are assured of its trustworthiness. This is our present question: Can we trust the Old Testament? A later chapter will similarly discuss the New Testament.

It is sometimes thought that a question of this kind is so technical as to be suitable only for scholars, and not for ordinary Christians. This, however, is not the view of many leading scholars themselves. Thus, Professor W. Robertson Smith, in his preface to a work by Wellhausen, says, "The present volume gives the English reader an opportunity to form his own judgment on questions which are within the scope of anyone who reads the English Bible carefully, and is able to think clearly and without prejudice about its contents." There are other criteria besides those of the expert. It is exactly the same with the Bible as it is with most other departments of life; scholarship is not everything, technicalities of learning cannot solve all problems. "There are more things in heaven and earth than are dreamt of" in human philosophy, and it is at once possible and a duty for the ordinary Christian to test the question of trustworthiness for himself. There are at least five ways of doing this. Each of them alone is important, but when they are taken together they are seen to provide the ordinary Christian with opportunities and methods of coming to a definite decision which is perfectly satisfying to the believing soul. The Bible is so vital and so important to the ordinary Christian man that unless he can be assured of its substantial trustworthiness as a record of divine revelation, his life and testimony must inevitably suffer. It is with the object of enabling him to arrive at this assurance for himself that these methods are indicated, and certain fundamental principles are enunciated.

1. *The Historical Fact of the Jewish Nation.*—The Jewish nation is a fact in history, and its

record is given to us in the Old Testament. There is no contemporary literature to check the account there given, and archeology only affords us assistance on points of detail, not for any long or continuous period. This record of Jewish history can be proved to have remained the same for many centuries, and what we find in the Old Testament agrees with all that is known from other sources.

Here before us we see the great outstanding objective fact of the Jewish nation. The Old Testament, as we have it, is at once the means and the record of their national life. It rose with them, grew with them, formed them, and at the same time witnessed against them, and it is to the Jews alone we look for the earliest testimony to the Old Testament canon.

In face of these historic facts, it is not too much to say that the trustworthiness of the Old Testament is wholly in accord with the historic growth and position of the Jewish people. And so we can test the Old Testament by the history of the Jews and find it in entire agreement with all that we know of Hebrew national life.

2. *The Evidence of Archeology.*—A vast number of discoveries have been made in Italy, Turkey, Greece, Egypt, Palestine, Assyria, and Babylonia, many of which have been valuable for their illustrations of the Bible. The special

advantage of these archeological results is that they are, as it were, tangible and intelligible by ordinary men and do not require expert scholarship to appreciate their meaning. The bearing of this on the Old Testament is obvious. It is impossible to adduce these discoveries in detail. And it is most striking and significant that not a single discovery has been made which goes to set aside or even weaken the trustworthiness of the Old Testament, while discovery after discovery has supported its statements.

3. *The Witness of our Lord and His Apostles.* —For many reasons I should prefer to leave the authority of our Lord out of this discussion, because I am convinced that scholarship is amply sufficient to settle the question. But while this is impossible, it is important to have a clear understanding of what it means to call attention to the evidence of the New Testament embodying the attitude of our Lord and his followers. We do not invoke the authority of Christ to close questions summarily, but we adduce the witness of the New Testament in support of the contentions of conservative historical scholarship. If we see that the witness of Christ and his apostles corresponds with the Church's view of the Bible, the testimony is assuredly weighty, and this is all that we claim.

What, then, was our Lord's general view of the

TRUSTWORTHINESS OF THE OLD TESTAMENT 51

Old Testament? That his Old Testament was practically, if not literally, the same as ours, and that he had a thorough knowledge of its contents, are admitted by all. Nor does any one seriously deny that Jesus Christ accepted the Old Testament as authoritative, inspired, and the final court of appeal for all questions connected with it. No one can go through the Gospels without being impressed with the profound reverence of our Lord for the Old Testament and with his constant use of it in all religious matters. Whether he referred to Bible names, or incidents, or to its deep teaching about God, it was always with the utmost reverence and with the evident conviction that it embodied a divine revelation. This general view is confirmed by his detailed references. His various testimonies to Old Testament persons imply their historical character. His references to the facts of the Old Covenant equally assume historicity. His whole earthly career was very largely a fulfilment of the Old Testament Scriptures.

4. *The Necessity of Spiritual Work.*—The use of the Bible in connection with Christian service is universally recognized, and the Old Testament part of it cannot be overlooked in work for God. Now no one doubts that the blessing of the Spirit of Truth rests upon those who are serving God while holding and teaching its trustworthi-

ness. There are men today of outstanding influence doing evangelistic and pastoral work who cling tenaciously to the "old paths." Their belief has been no bar to the grace of God. Blessing has manifestly come through use of the books of the Old Testament as they now exist. Divine lessons have been brought home to us by means of the present form of the older part of Scripture. While we welcome all that scholarship can do in making the past clearer, and in enabling us to enter more fully into the divine methods of work, yet the Bible is the revelation of God for spiritual life, and not merely for historical literature, however valuable. Whenever scholarship tends to forget this, the question of the spiritual value of the Bible becomes imperative.

For this reason we hold that any doctrine of the Bible for spiritual men must bear the seal of the Holy Spirit. The view of its trustworthiness has the mark of this seal, and has been, abundantly blessed.

5. *The Testimony of Spiritual Experience.* — There is one special way of testing this matter, for truth requires verification by the spiritual man. When the divine Word is brought to bear upon the human mind, conscience, heart and will, it carries its own conviction and elicits its own verification. The experience of the soul soon bears witness in the words of the Psalmist, "Thy

TRUSTWORTHINESS OF THE OLD TESTAMENT 53

Word is a lamp unto my feet, and a light unto my path" (Psa. 119:105). "Thy Word is very pure: Therefore Thy servant loveth it" (Psa. 119:140).

We ask for an earnest and thorough consideration of these five tests. It would have been possible to add others more technical and more directly applicable to questions of scholarship, but these will suffice to show how the ordinary Christian man can test the trustworthiness of the Old Testament Scriptures. When these tests are applied separately they will be seen to carry real weight, but when they are taken together they constitute a cumulative effect and demand attention from all who seek to know the truth.

QUESTIONS

1. What is the fundamental question about the Bible?
2. Is the question of the trustworthiness of the Old Testament one that can be answered by any but scholars?
3. In how many ways may this question of trustworthiness be tested?
4. What is the relation of the Jewish nation to the Old Testament? What is the source, very largely, of that nation's history?
5. In what way have archeological discoveries been valuable to Bible students?
6. What has been the bearing of these discoveries on the question of the trustworthiness of the Old Testament?
7. In what way is the witness of Christ to the Old Testament invoked?
8. What was our Lord's attitude to the Old Testament?
9. How is the trustworthiness of the Old Testament shown practically in work for God?

10. How may this trustworthiness be brought home convincingly to the average Christian?

6

TRUSTWORTHINESS OF THE NEW TESTAMENT

THE PRIMARY QUESTION concerning the New Testament, the one on which all else rests, must never be forgotten. It is the same one that has already been faced in relation to the Old Testament; viz., its historical trustworthiness. Is it an accurate presentation? This must and can be tested at every point, and the following constitute the main avenues of approach.

1. *The Gospels.* — The record is specially noteworthy on account of something that is apt to be overlooked. It is well known that in the entire realm of literature there is no trace of the picture of a perfect character. Poets, novelists, dramatists, philosophers, essayists, have given

the world wonderful creations and yet no writer has ever attempted to portray a perfect man or woman. Professor Mackintosh has said that Tennyson's King Arthur is one of the most recent failures in this respect. And yet in the Gospels, written by ordinary men, not literary geniuses, we have a perfect character depicted. How did the Evangelists accomplish what no writer has ever attempted with success? As Fairbairn asked, did the record invent the Person or did the Person create the record? It has often been pointed out that if the four Evangelists invented the character of Jesus Christ we are faced with a literary miracle of the first magnitude. There is only one explanation of the literary features of the Gospels; their presentation of Christ is true.

The same result is seen by a consideration of his character in detail. What are we to say of the unique feature of Christ's sinlessness? How is it that only one man has been found out of all the millions of the world's history in whom the entail of sin has been broken? Then, too, what is to be said about the marvelous combination and equally wonderful balance of qualities found in Jesus which are seldom found in their blend and never found in their balance in any one else? No wonder that Bushnell should say that "the character of Jesus Christ forbids his possible classification with men."

TRUSTWORTHINESS OF THE NEW TESTAMENT

The claim of Christ as recorded in the Gospel is another point of great importance. He claimed to be perfect (John 8:46); to be the Jewish Messiah (Matt. 26:64); to be the Master of mankind (Matt. 4:19); to be the Judge of the world (Matt. 25:32); to exercise the prerogatives of God (Matt. 28:20; Mark 2:10; John 9:38). How are these claims to be explained? Rabbi Duncan said the last word when he put it thus: "Christ either deceived mankind by conscious fraud; or was Himself deluded and self-deceived, or He was Divine."

Taking the record of the life of Jesus in the Gospels, no one can seriously doubt the consistency of the picture and the persistence of it in spite of all the acute criticism.

2. *The Book of Acts.*—This record of the first thirty years of the history of the Christian community has been the subject of much and thorough examination of late years, and, as is well known, the great scholarship of Sir William Ramsay has endorsed its accuracy in the light of archeological research in Asia Minor and elsewhere. In addition to its representations of the primitive Christian society, the book comes into contact at several points with the secular history of Palestine, Greece and Rome, and the result of testing it confirms our conviction that Luke was

a first-rate historian and can be relied on for accuracy.

3. *The Christian Church.* — The New Testament gives the record of the commencement of the society which we call the Church. A few people believed that their Master was alive, and formed themselves in a society based on this conviction. Then they set out to proclaim this as a message; and wherever they went the same result followed, societies sprang up believing Jesus Christ was alive. But this often meant opposition, stern and persistent; it almost always involved persecution, cruel and relentless; it frequently led to death. But, in spite of all, the Church continued, increased, and extended far and wide. No temporal advantage led men to join it; no human force compelled them to become associated with it. The Church everywhere consisted of free, loyal, devoted adherents whose relation to Christ impelled them to continue their testimony of word and deed to the Master whom they trusted and loved.

This is the society of which the start and early years found their record in the New Testament. And is it not instinct with reality?

4. *The Apostle Paul.* — The character and career of Paul afford a special opportunity of testing the trustworthiness of the New Testament. As a man he was of outstanding force, a

man of great intellectual ability, of intense feeling, of keen conscientiousness, and of strong, determined will. When mind, emotion, conscience and will combine, as they did in Saul of Tarsus, we have a real man, one in the very front rank. Now it was this able man that became a persecutor of Christians and, using his own language, was "exceedingly mad against them." He went into houses, dragged out men and women, put them into prison, simply because they were Christians. Then, when he went to Damascus, a hundred and fifty miles away, to continue the work, something happened, and the persecutor became a preacher of the very faith he had formerly attempted to destroy. Not only so, but he continued in the same course for thirty years amid opposition, persecutions, perils, and disappointments. How are we to account for Saul's conversion and Paul's apostleship? Baur examined this problem some years ago, and confessed it was insoluble. So with every theory since then; they have been shattered on the simple rock of Paul's historical testimony, "It pleased God to reveal his Son in me." And what is this but a striking proof of the trustworthiness of the New Testament?

5. *The Agreement with the Old Testament.*—We hardly realize that the New Testament is not a book, but twenty-seven books, and the remark-

able feature is that these twenty-seven books proceeding from eight authors are in absolute unity with the thirty-nine books of the Old Testament. That book is one of (1) Prophecies largely unfulfilled; (2) Ceremonies mainly unexplained; (3) Aspirations mostly unsatisfied. But the New Testament meets these three features of incompleteness with its three lines of teaching. (1) The Prophecies are fulfilled in Jesus the Prophet. (2) The Ceremonies are explained in Jesus Christ the Sacrifice and Priest. (3) The Aspirations are satisfied in Jesus Christ the Lord — "Jesus my Prophet, Priest, and King." Could the agreement have been due to the collusion of all the eight writers of the New Testament? Impossible. As the great Methodist theologian, Dr. W. B. Pope, well said:

> That the New Testament as fulfilment should so perfectly correspond with the Old Testament as prophecy is in itself the most wonderful phenomenon in literature: it is evidence as near demonstration as needs be of the intervention of a divine Hand. The Redeemer made manifest in the later Scripture answers face to face, and feature for feature, to the Form predicted in the older Scripture. One idea runs through the whole: the kingdom of God set up or restored in His Incarnate Son.

6. *The Unique Claim.* — For the first two or

TRUSTWORTHINESS OF THE NEW TESTAMENT 61

three hundred years Christianity suffered persecution at the hands of the Roman Empire. This was because it claimed to dispossess every other religious system and to be the only religion in the world. If the Christian people had gone to the Emperor and others in authority and said. "This is a new religion; we want you to allow it to come with the others and be put in your Pantheon," they would have been ready to allow Christianity to appear as one of the number. But that was not the way of the Gospel. It said, in effect, "No, this is the only religion. The others are not religions." Persecution then came upon Christianity, because it was intolerant — in the right sense of the word, the only way in which any one has a right to be intolerant, with the intolerance of truth.

Another point of great importance is included in this claim. The Bible has now been before the world for nearly two thousand years in its complete form, and yet it has said the last word on the greatest things in life. We find in it the last word about God, the last word about salvation from sin, the last word about holiness, the last word about the future life. And as has often been pointed out, while we outgrow the teaching of other men, we never outgrow the teaching of Jesus Christ and his apostles.

Not only so, we have had great systems of

philosophy and morality during the last thousand or fifteen hundred years, great theories, great books, and great ideas: but there is not a single new moral fact, not a single new ethical truth, in any one of these great systems that we cannot find in this Book. How is it that with all the great teachers of these centuries nothing new and true has been propounded beyond what is found in this Book?

Surely the claim of Christ and his apostles to finality is true. "No man cometh unto the Father but by me" (John 14:6). "In none other is there salvation: for neither is there any other name under heaven, that is given among men, wherein we must be saved." And these claims, if true, support the historical trustworthiness of the New Testament.

7. *The Spiritual Power.* — For most Christian people the simplest and most conclusive proof of the Bible will be that which is derived from their own use of Holy Scripture in daily life and work. First and foremost, Scripture is a spiritual book brought home to the heart by the Holy Spirit, and it is just here that criticism fails us. A learned writer justly says:

> I am struck with the absence of any sign of an experience distinctively Christian in many of those who discuss the sanctuaries of the Chris-

Trustworthiness of the New Testament 63

tian faith . . . Some of these scholars, to judge from their writings alone, do not seem even so much as to have heard of a Holy Ghost. And they have a fatal dread of pietism, and methodism, and most forms of intensely personal evangelical faith. They are, like Haeckel, in their own way the victims of an intellectualism which means spiritual atrophy to Christianity at last.

In matters of the soul it is better to have the dogma of the telescope than that of the microscope. It is better to have the dogma of Melancthon, or even Calvin, than of Wellhausen or Schmiedel (whom I name with due respect for the great work they represent). The one has the positivity of infinite revelation, the other the positivism of the present age.

Taking these seven considerations together, can there be any real doubt or serious question about the historical accuracy and therefore trustworthiness of the New Testament? And if we proceed to enquire as to the cause of this reliability, there is only one explanation: the New Testament is a supernatural book.

QUESTIONS

1. What one feature makes the Gospels noteworthy? In this respect how do they compare with literature generally?
2. What explanation of the literary features of the Gospels is alone possible? State Principal Fairbairn's dictum on this question.

3. How is this seen to be true when Christ's character is studied in detail? How did Rabbi Duncan sum up the possibilities concerning Christ?
4. What has been the result of the examination into the accuracy of the Book of the Acts? Whose work is largely responsible for this result?
5. In what way does the Christian Church establish the accuracy of the New Testament?
6. Who is the most outstanding man in the New Testament? How do his life and experience give a special opportunity for testing its trustworthiness?
7. What is the New Testament? Is it in harmony with the Old Testament? What very largely is the character of the Old Testament? How is this met in the New Testament?
8. What is the nature of Christianity's claim? What was the attitude of the Roman Empire toward Christianity as a consequence of this claim?
9. What is the character of the pronouncements of the Bible, touching God, man, salvation, and other subjects?
10. What will most people regard as the simplest and most conclusive proof of the trustworthiness of the Bible?

7

UNITY OF THE BIBLE

VERY OFTEN we fail to realize that the Bible is not a book, but a library. The word "Bible" really suggests that, if we happen to know that while it is now applied to one book it comes from a Greek term meaning "the books" — *ta biblia*. An edition of the Bible in various volumes, with one allotted to Genesis, another to Exodus, and on through the Bible, helps us to realize that it is a library, not merely a volume. Yet notwithstanding all these sixty-six books, there is a real unity running through it from Genesis to Revelation, constituting one of the most impressive features connected with our belief in the Bible as the Word of God.

1. *The Fact of Unity.* — This unity can be

realized all the more clearly if we first think of the variety of the Bible. There is variety of contents — history, theology, philosophy, poetry, counsel, aspiration, prediction. There is variety of authorship — prophet, priest, king, annalist, apostle, evangelist. There is variety of circumstances — differences of time, place, country, purpose, destination. The sixty-six books are the work of at least thirty-six to forty authors, and cover certainly sixteen centuries. And yet the Bible, though so varied, is essentially one, and possesses one predominant idea. The Old Testament is the product of one country, though stretching over a long period of time. The New Testament is the product of several countries, but extending over a short time. The Old is to the New as the foundation is to the structure, and the New to the Old as the building is to the base. The God of Genesis and the God of Matthew are the same, only with the two complementary aspects of transcendence and immanence. In the Old Testament we have God in Himself as supreme, while in the New we have God in Christ as our Saviour. In the Old Testament man is seen in himself as a sinner. In the New he is seen in Christ as saved. To quote some familiar words, "In the Old the New is concealed (latent), and in the New the Old is revealed (patent)."

UNITY OF THE BIBLE

2. *The Unity of Purpose.*—The one purpose of the Bible from beginning to end is to record God's religion of redemption. Dr. M. G. Kyle once helpfully stated this by pointing out that in the Patriarchs we have the promise of redemption; in the time of the Judges, the Providence which was leading to redemption; in the period of the monarchy, the prophecies of redemption; in Christ the Person who wrought redemption; in the Acts and Epistles the preaching of redemption; and in Revelation the prediction which was the outcome of redemption.

In view of this great purpose it may be said that the Old Testament is a revelation of outward forms developing inward principles, while the New is a revelation of inward principles developing outward forms. The former is suited to moral and spiritual childhood, and the latter to moral and spiritual adulthood. The Old Testament is thus a preparation of Christ for the Church and of the Church for Christ. The New is a revelation of Christ to the Church, and through the Church to the world.

3. *The Unity of Subject.*—It is a familiar story, but is worth repeating, that the late Dr. A. J. Gordon, of Boston, on one occasion was in his study with some of his children, and gave them a puzzle, one of those made of different sized pieces of wood, which have to be properly fitted

together. He went out and came back unexpectedly soon afterward, when to his surprise, he found the puzzle already completed. He asked his children how they had managed to do it so soon, and one of them replied: "We saw a picture of a man on the back and this helped us to know where the pieces were to go." And so, as it has often been pointed out, there is a picture of a man, the man Christ Jesus, anticipated in the Old Testament, and realized in the New, and this gives unity to the Book.

Christ is thus the key to the whole Bible, and gives it its historical and spiritual unity. The following unity which covers the whole Bible has been suggested and is well worth consideration:

1. Genesis to Deuteronomy — Revelation.
2. Joshua to Esther — Preparation.
3. Job to Song of Solomon — Aspiration.
4. Isaiah to Malachi — Expectation.
5. Matthew to John — Manifestation.
6. Acts to Epistles — Realization.
7. Revelation — Culmination.

Of course these are only to be understood quite generally, but they are sufficiently accurate to reveal the essential unity.

4. *The Unity of Theme.* — It is said on good authority that every piece of rope in the British

UNITY OF THE BIBLE 69

Navy has a red thread running through it, so that it may be safeguarded against theft. Wherever that rope is cut the red thread can be seen. In the same way there is a "red thread" running through the Bible, and wherever we examine it, we see indications of that "thread" in the unity of theme running from Genesis to Revelation. The "red thread" is only another expression for the Cross of Christ. In the Old Testament that Cross is *promised* in prophecy and *pictured* in sacrifice and personal types (Acts 8:34, 35). In the Gospels it appeared gradually in the teaching of Christ, and was at length *provided* in the event on Calvary (John 1:29). In the Acts the Cross is *proclaimed* in sermons and explanations (2:23; 3:15; 4:10; 5:30; 7:52; 10:39, 40; 23:29, 30). In the Epistles it is *proved* in various ways, and shown in its theological and practical bearings (Eph. 1:7). Then in Revelation it is *praised* as theme of the glorified saints whose one song is "Worthy the Lamb that was slain" (5:6; 13:8).

5. *The Unity as seen in the Symmetry.*—This symmetry is characteristic both of the literary structure and also of the spiritual teaching of the Bible. The shortest expression of it is that in the Old Testament we have Moses and the prophets, and in the New, Christ and his apostles.

Extending this somewhat further, we may notice that the Pentateuch is to the Old Testament what the Gospels are to the New, the foundation on which all else rests, so that it may be regarded as generally correct to say that the Pentateuch and Gospels are books of the revelation of God to man, and the rest of the Old and New Testaments are books of the realization of that revelation in man. This can be made clearer if put in tabular form.

1. *Revelation* (Pentateuch). God to his people.
2. *Realization* (Rest of the Old Testament). God in his people.

   (1) *In outward expression*. Historical books.
   (2) *In inward experience*. Poetical books.
   (3) *In onward expectation*. Prophetical books.

Taking the New Testament in the same way we have

1. *Revelation* (Gospels). Christ to his Church.
2. *Realization* (Rest of the New Testament). Christ in his Church.

   (1) *In outward expression* (History). Acts.
   (2) *In inward experience* (Doctrine). Epistles.
   (3) *In onward expectation* (Prophecy). Revelation.

There are other and fuller ways of seeing the wonderful symmetry of the Word of God, but these will suffice to show something of its wonderful unitary structure.

UNITY OF THE BIBLE

This unity is one of the unique features of the Bible that nothing in scholarship or anything else can destroy. Some words on this point were quoted in Chapter VI from a great Methodist theologian, Dr. W. B. Pope.

Here is another statement from him:

"The unity of Scripture is a very strong credential in its favor as professing to be from God. It is one great vision, and its interpretation one: beginning and ending with the same paradise, with thousands of years of redeeming history between . . . One idea runs through the whole: the kingdom of God set up or restored in his Incarnate Son. To this idea authors of various ages and of various races contribute in harmony which never could be the result of accident or mere coincidence. Only the divine Power could have made so many men of different lands concert, yet without concerting, such a scheme of literature. If they had not asserted their inspiration of God, that hypothesis would have had to be invented to account for the facts and phenomena of their writings. But they have asserted it: the claim is bound up with every page of the Word they have left behind them."

All this inevitably compels the question as to how a unity of this kind is possible, and there is only one answer. Some years ago while a tunnel was being constructed in London, five shafts were sunk, and ten sets of men worked toward each other from opposite directions. Ultimately the sets met in the middle of the tunnel at a depth of one hundred feet. They were working practically in the dark, but they fitted so well together when the tunnels met each other that every one could see there was a master-mind who had planned the whole thing. And so the various writers of the Old and New Testaments were working separately, as it were, in a tunnel in the dark, and the apostle Peter tells us they did not know exactly the meaning of their own words (1 Pet. 1:11). But by and by they met, and now that we have the Bible complete, the writers are seen to have worked together and to have dovetailed into one another, thus showing the presence and power of a master-mind, which is none other than that of the Holy Spirit of God.

QUESTIONS

1. What may the Bible properly be called? How is this suggested by the name "Bible"?
2. How may the Bible's unity be clearly realized?
3. What is the one purpose of the Bible throughout? In view of this, how may the two parts of Scripture be described?
4. What gives unity to the Bible? What is the key to it? How may this be shown graphically?
5. May it be said that there is a unity of theme running through the Bible? What is the theme? How may this be strikingly illustrated?

Unity of the Bible

6. In what characteristic of the Bible is its unity seen? In what two respects is this characteristic observable?
7. What relation do the Pentateuch and the Gospels bear to the remainder of the Old and New Testaments?
8. What, therefore may be properly asserted?
9. Write graphically the answer to the last question.
10. What does Dr. Pope assert with respect to inspiration?

8

PROGRESSIVENESS OF THE BIBLE

IT IS OFTEN THOUGHT that belief in the unity of Scripture carries with it the inevitable conclusion that everything in it is on the same level of spiritual value, that the teaching and authority (say) of Ecclesiastes are not essentially lower than those of (say) Ephesians. But this idea of uniform spiritual value is assuredly not a logical consequence of a belief in the unity of the Bible. On the contrary, just as in the human body, some members are more important than others, and yet each is necessary in its place and for its purpose, so in the Bible, some parts are of less, and others are of greater spiritual importance and value. The two truths of the Unity and

Progressiveness of Scripture must, therefore, be held together, and the latter must be allowed to explain and vindicate the former.

1. *The Principle.* — The Bible consists of two parts, Old Testament and New Testament, and in these it is possible to see the general progress of truth. The former indicates Law, and the latter Grace. The one deals for the most part with rules suited to moral childhood, the other, with principles applicable to moral maturity.

But within these two main divisions there are still further and fuller instances of progress. God has revealed his will to man in many parts and in many ways (Heb. 1:1), and it is usual to speak of these as dispensations, meaning particular methods of the divine attitude and action. While in general we speak of the Jewish and Christian dispensations, we can and must go into further detail, and notice both in the Old Testament and in the New, the different yet connected stages of God's revelation to man. Some students suggest seven of these dispensations: the Edenic; the Antediluvian; the Patriarchal; the Mosaic; the Christian; the Millennial and the Eternal. Even these are capable of fuller division, for the Mosaic dispensation can be distinguished as the Theocracy (the time from Egypt to Samuel); the Monarchy (from Saul to the Captivity); and the Return (from the restoration to Malachi). The

PROGRESSIVENESS OF THE BIBLE 77

Christian dispensation can be similarly divided into the times before and after Pentecost.

Now in these various divisions it is often possible to distinguish God's manifestation of himself and of his truth at different stages. There was a gradually increasing expression of the divine character and will at successive periods, just as the people were considered ready to receive it. This means that while the revelation at every stage or dispensation was perfect for its own time, it was not necessarily suited for a following stage.

Now, however, we may divide the periods, it is clear that a distinction of this kind has to be drawn. Thus, when Christ said, "I have many things to say unto you, but ye cannot bear them now" (John 16:12), He was indicating, what I am now emphasizing, that truth was progressive and not all delivered at once. For, as the Lord went on to say, "howbeit when he, the Spirit of truth, is come, he will guide you into all truth."

Other proofs of the same gradual unfolding of the complete revelation of God for man, can be seen in these two instances. In the Sermon on the Mount, Christ first declared the Old Testament truth, and then supplemented and deepened it by adding, "but I say unto you" (Matt. 5:17-48). And it is clear from Mark 16:17-20, when five miraculous signs are said to "follow them that believe," that the reference cannot be to the present period of the Church (for these signs do not "follow them that believe"), but to that transitional period comprised in the thirty years of the Book of the Acts, during which time the Gospel was being offered to the Jews, and when we have the record of four of the five "signs" plainly stated as having "followed them that believe."

But in all this progressiveness of revelation, it is necessary and important to remember that it did not involve any *repudiation* of what had gone before. Like the repealing of a law which is in force up to the time of the repeal, the teaching for each stage was valid and obligatory until supplemented and thereby supplanted by fresh and fuller instruction. But repeal of a law never means repudiation, only a "disannulling" because of a completer provision (Heb. 7:18).

A striking proof of this has been shown in the fact that there are traces in Scripture of later portions carrying an endorsement of previous stages. Joshua confirms the law of Moses (Josh. 1:8). The first Psalm emphasizes the value of the law (v. 2). Acts refers back to the third Gospel. The Old Testament is frequently endorsed in the New. Throughout the Old Testament there are, as we have already seen, traces of the gradual growth by accretion of the various books, until the Canon was complete. All this attestation of one part of Scripture by another is a proof at once of its unity and its progressiveness. Then, at length we have the meridian of truth in the New Testament revelation.

2. *The Principle Illustrated.*—Out of many examples of this progressiveness of revelation, two will be adduced. The first is the doctrine of God. In the Old Testament emphasis is rightly placed on the unity of the Godhead as against the "gods many" of heathenism. But in the New Testament there is the additional revelation of the Trinity, which is not only not contradictory of the Unity, but is based on it and developed out of it. Every one knows that the Christian doctrine of the Trinity never had the slightest connection with polytheism, but grew out of Jewish monotheism. It is significant that with all the Jewish objections to Christianity in Paul's time, no trace can be found of any opposition to his doctrine of a distinction between the Deity of the Father and the Deity of the Son, which was the germ of the fully-developed doctrine of the Trinity.

The explanation of this was that the Jewish believers, having been led by experience into an acceptance of Christ as a divine Redeemer (and thereby to a distinction in the Deity) found in their Old Testament anticipatory hints of the

Trinity. They realized that the unity of the Godhead was compound not simple, as the Hebrew words for "one" clearly indicate (Deut. 6:4; Exod. 26:6-11; Ezek. 37:16-19).

Another illustration of the progressiveness of revelation is seen in the difference between the morality of the Old and New Testaments. This doctrine of the progress of revelation helps us to distinguish between God's temporary and permissive will and his absolute and inflexible standard. The former is seen in the Old Testament and the latter in the New Testament, and as we study the first-named we can see in it clear indications of its temporary character. Thus, while permitting slavery, restrictions were imposed, and cruelty was prohibited (Exod. 21:16-27). Many of the Old Testament difficulties can be solved, or at least relieved, by the consideration of this purely temporary and merely permissive character of the morality. Christ referred to this when he distinguished between the primal divine command about marriage, and the Mosaic toleration of divorce (Matt. 19:8).

This principle of progress in God's revelation is of great practical service in meeting certain current objections to the Old Testament. There are those who reject it because of its alleged cruelties, such as the slaughter of the Canaanites, or because of certain manifestations in individual life and practise not consonant with New Testament principles. Now, while we are not to be guided today by many of the examples of the Old Testament, it is equally true that *in so far as what they said and did was due to a revelation of God, that revelation was perfect for that time,* whatever additional truth came afterward for newer needs. We say *in so far as what they said and did was of God,* because not even in the Old Testament are we to understand that God necessarily approved of *all* that his servants said and did, even when they thought they were doing him service. But if this were the place to do it, the instance of the Canaanites, already referred to, could be justified, without much difficulty, in the light of the divine judgment on the awful depths of sin to which they had descended (Gen. 15:16).

There is another point that is too apt to be overlooked, namely, that side by side with the gradual development of God's revelation there was an equally gradual deterioration of Israel, so that they in their degeneration failed to realize and respond to the ever-enlarging disclosure of God. And so it has been well pointed out that "there are no set-backs in the revelation made to Israel, but there are many set-backs in the religious history of Israel." It is the failure to recognize this distinction between the divine and the human that has caused people to regard Old Testament morality as low and unworthy of God, when all the time the explanation has been in the failure of the people to accept the growing truth of God. This is how the distinction has been put:

"In regard to the Old Testament I suggest two words of guiding principle: 'The Law of the Lord is perfect' (that is, its quality). 'The Law made nothing perfect' (that is, its achievement — in its office as a preparatory discipline to 'school' souls for Christ). These two statements can be written across the sacred Record. A perfect revelation — imperfect faith. Perfect ethical requirement — imperfect obedience."

And so, God revealed himself, not only at "sundry times" but also in "divers manners," to the fathers. He taught men as they were able to bear it. He led them step by step from the dawn of revelation up to the fulness and splendor of his manifestation "in these last days in his Son" (Heb. 1:2). A knowledge of this principle of progress in God's revelation of himself will enable us to avoid a twofold error: it will prevent us, on the one hand, from undervaluing the Old Testament by reason of our fuller light from the New Testament; on the other hand, it will prevent us from using the Old Testament in any of its stages without guidance from the complete revelation in Christ. We shall thereby be enabled to obtain the correct spiritual perspective from which to study the Old Testament, and to derive from it the wealth of spiritual instruction it was intended to convey to all ages (Rom. 15:4).

We have thus to distinguish carefully between what may be called *temporary* teaching and *permanent* truth in the Old Testament—that is, between those elements of God's revelation intended solely for the immediate need, and those which are of eternal validity. To put it in yet another way, we have to remember the difference between what is written *to* us and *for* us. All Scripture was written *for our learning*, but not all was written *to* us directly. Much of it was not addressed to Christians but to Jews, and was primarily and often exclusive for them, and is only for us today by way of application. This distinction will solve many a difficulty and the progress of doctrine is one of the masterkeys of the Bible.

QUESTIONS

1. Does the fact of the unity of Scripture indicate that all parts of it are of equal value?
2. What two great truths must be held together when studying the Bible?
3. What are the main divisions of the Bible? Are there any subdivisions in these main divisions? Suggest one.

4. Give one other proof of the gradual unfolding of the complete revelation. Does the idea of progressiveness of revelation involve the repudiation of what has gone before? Prove your answer.
5. How is God revealed in the Old Testament? Why? How is he revealed in the New Testament?
6. How is the progressiveness of revelation seen in the difference in the ethical teaching of the Old and New Testaments?
7. How may many Old Testament difficulties be solved? What practical value has this principle?
8. By what principle are the words and deeds of Old Testament characters to be judged?
9. What principle was working in Israel while God's revelation was unfolding?
10. What two words describe the Old and New Testaments? What error will a knowledge of this principle of progressiveness of revelation help us to avoid? Distinguish between "temporary" and "permanent truth" as used in relation to the Old Testament.

9

INSPIRATION OF THE BIBLE

THE BASIS of our acceptance of the Bible is the belief that it embodies a divine revelation. But at once the question arises as to how the authority of this revelation is expressed. This brings us to the problem of Inspiration.

At the outset two things should be said: (1) If we accept the Authority of Scripture we really need not trouble about any particular theory of Inspiration, but (2) if we seek to know as fully as we can what Inspiration means we should confine ourselves strictly to facts, since Inspiration when properly understood is not a theory, but a fact. It is something we accept, whether we can explain it or not.

1. *The Source of the Bible.*—We believe that the Bible comes from a divine Source. The Old Testament prophets claimed to be the recipients of divine revelation. "The word of the Lord came"; "the Lord spake"; "the word of God"; "God said"; "the Lord commanded." Phrases like these are found nearly seven hundred times in the Pentateuch alone, and they are scattered throughout the Scriptures no less than three thousand times altogether. There is one verse, which, whatever else it means, certainly makes this plain: 2 Samuel 23: 2, "The Spirit of the Lord spake by me, and his word was on my tongue."

In harmony with this, we have a claim in the New Testament, of the presence and power of the Holy Spirit. In some passages there is no reference to the human writer of the Scripture, but only to the divine Author. In Hebrews 3: 7, we read, "The Holy Spirit saith." This refers to Psalm 95, which was, of course, written by a man, David or someone else, and yet there is no reference at all to a human author. This use shows that the writer is concerned, not with what the Psalmist said, but with the Holy Spirit's utterances, and this means that the Holy Spirit is the Author of Scripture.

The attitude of the New Testament to the Old Testament shows the same truth. Over fifty times in the New Testament, is the Old Testament spoken of as of divine origin and authority, and always with the deference due to this fact (Rom. 3:2; Matt. 22:29; Mark 14:49; Luke 24:25-27, 44-46).

2. *The Instruments of the Bible.*—The Holy Spirit used men as the instruments of divine revelation. There are a number of passages where the divine and the human are mentioned; where the distinction is drawn very clearly between the divine Author and the human instrument. Thus in Matthew 1:22, we have "Spoken of the Lord by the prophet," in Acts 1:16, "The Holy Ghost spake by the mouth of David," and in 2 Peter 1:21, "Holy men of old spake as they were moved [carried along] by the Holy Ghost." So that as the instruments of the Spirit's work, the men were first the speakers, and then the writers of divine revelation. And yet "instrument" does not mean passivity, as "pens," but rather, the thought is expressed by the word in the case of *penmen*. Inspiration is a *concursus* of the divine and human.

3. *The Media of the Bible.* — I do not know any other term than this that will better express my idea. I mean the words of the men (2 Pet. 1:21). The men themselves are not alive now, and if we are to be in touch with their revelation, it must be through their words; and if we are to be sure of the revelation from God, then for us today

we must be sure of what the men wrote, as they are not here to speak for themselves.

Let us notice 2 Timothy 3:16. Whether we follow the Authorized Version or the Revised Version, the thought is: "Every writing is God-breathed." God, somehow or other, breathed into these writings and therefore we are concerned with words.

Now look at 1 Corinthians 2:13. Dr. Forsyth says the chapter is classic for the apostolic view of inspiration. Mark this: *"Words* which the Holy Ghost teacheth." Could anything be more definite and clear than this? Not the words which man's wisdom teacheth, but the *words* which "the Holy Ghost teacheth." And so there is an intimate, a necessary connection, between thoughts and words. Whether it be for our own thinking, or for intercourse between man and man, thoughts must be expressed in words. And this is exactly what Bishop Westcott says in his Essay on Inspiration! "Thoughts are wedded to words as necessarily as soul is to body." So when we speak of the *media* of the Bible, we are concerned with words.

But some one says: Does not this mean "verbal inspiration"? Well, we can call it verbal inspiration if we like, or we can call it plenary inspiration, if we prefer, so long as we do not call it dictation. When a man dictates a letter to his

INSPIRATION OF THE BIBLE 89

secretary, he does not inspire her. It is mechanical dictation, and he expects her to reproduce exactly what he tells her. But in Scripture we do not have mechanical dictation, but inspiration; and whether we call it verbal or plenary, the phrase is not intended to say *how* God does it, but *how far* it has gone. It means that inspiration extends to the form as well as to the substance, that *it reaches to the words as well as to the thoughts,* in order that we may be sure of the thoughts; for how are we to know God's thoughts if we do not know his words? God used the natural characteristics of the writers, and through them conveyed his truth.

But does it not say: "The letter killeth, the spirit giveth life"? It does; but in that phrase Paul is not concerned with the letter of inspiration as opposed to the spirit. That is an entirely false idea of the passage. Again someone says: "We want the inspiration of the thoughts, not of the words." Now, what do we really mean by inspiration or authority in the thoughts? Surely this must be expressed in the words, and the objections raised to the inspiration of words are just as valid against the inspiration of thoughts.

Surely inspiration cannot mean an uninspired account of inspired thoughts. How did Moses remember God's revelation found in Exodus 25 to 30, or Isaiah remember that which is found in chapters 8 to 12, or Hosea remember the contents of chapters 4 to 11? As these are evidently continuous revelations, are we to rely on the writers' memory only, and on no other faculty? As Dr. Kuyper has truly said: "You can as easily have music without notes or mathematics without figures as thoughts without words."

Let us notice 1 Corinthians 14:37, "If any man think himself to be spiritual, let him acknowledge that the things I write are the commandments of the Lord." Here we see both the human instrument and the divine authority.

This is how Dr. A. T. Pierson has put the matter:

"There are, with regard to this question of verbal inspiration, or the oversight of the very words of Scripture, five important significant passages in the Word of God: Hebrews 12:27; Galatians 4:9; John 8:58; John 10:34-36; Galatians 3:16. If these passages are examined it will be seen that in the first instance the argument turns on *one phrase*, 'yet once more.' In the second, on the *passive voice* rather than the *active voice* of the verb. In the third, on the *present* rather than on the *past* tense. In the fourth, on the inviolability of a single *word;* and in the fifth, on the retention of the *singular number of a noun*, rather than the plural. Taking the five passages together, they teach us that, to alter or omit a phrase, change the voice or mood or tense of a verb, change a single word or even the number of a noun, is to break the Scriptures; and if this does not come close to verbal inspiration, then I am no judge."

The use of the Bible today is a wonderful confirmation of this view. We regard it as our authoritative court of appeal, and we rest upon its words as our warrant, and the fact that we employ a concordance, be it Greek, or Hebrew, or English, is another testimony to this belief. It points to the value, the meaning, the force, and the extent of words.

This was the view of the Apostolic Church. Bishop Westcott, in the Essay to which I have already referred, says that the doctrine of inspiration as held in the Apostolic churches was that it was supernatural in source, unerring in truthfulness, and that it comprised words as well as subject-matter. This, according to the Bishop, is the view of the earliest churches, and certainly it has also been that of a great many churches since the Apostolic days.

We notice, too, the precise form of the appeal of the New Testament to the Old: "It is *written*." It is not "it is *thought*," or "it is *suggested*," but, "it is *written*." And the Lord Himself said, in John 10: 35, "The *Scripture* cannot be broken." So we are on perfectly safe ground when we ask attention to *the words* of Scripture as the *media* of the men who spake by the Holy Ghost.

As Dr. J. H. Brookes used to say about Exodus 4:10-12, it is not, "I will be with thy mind and teach thee what thou shalt think," but "I will be with thy mouth and teach thee what thou shalt say," because while it does not so much matter what Moses thought, it *does* matter what he actually said.

4. *The Substance of the Bible.*—What is the outcome of this Source, these instruments and media? *Truth.* This is the substance of the Bible. First of all, truth in its reality. The greatest authority we have, the Lord Jesus, once said, "*Thy Word* is truth." Truth in its reality is found in this book. As Dr. Denney remarks, "When a man submits his mind to the Spirit which is in the Bible, it never misleads him about the way of salvation, it brings him invariably to that knowledge of God which is eternal life. The most vital truth about it is covered by the terms inspiration and infallibility, and in virtue of this truth it is indispensable and authoritative to the mind of every age."

Secondly, Truth in its uniqueness. We can test the work of the Holy Spirit in regard to the Bible very simply. Take the writings of A.D. 50 to 100. Then take the writings from A.D. 100 to 150. Compare them, and, as it has been well said, between the New Testament writings of A.D. 50 to 100, and the most post-apostolic writings of A.D. 100 to 150, there is a chasm, "sheer, deep, and abysmal." The finest writings of the second century cannot compare with the writings of the first century. When the Christian faith was settling itself in the world, the Holy Spirit was working in a unique manner. He was at work as the Spirit of inspiration. But from A.D. 100 to 150 we do not have inspiration; but illumination. From that time forward, and ever since, there has been constant illumination, but no new revelation. John Robinson, of Leyden, said: "The Lord hath yet more light and truth to break forth from His Word." True, but it is from *His Word*. We have not reached the end of it yet, but there it is, ready for the Holy Spirit to illuminate its pages. What does all this involve but the fact of a divine, unique inspiration?

QUESTIONS

1. What is the basis of our acceptance of the Bible?
2. Is any particular theory of inspiration important if the authority of the Bible be accepted? What is inspiration?
3. What is the source of the Bible?
4. Who were the instruments of divine revelation? What thought is conveyed in the use of the word instrument?
5. What are the media of the Bible? Explain this usage of the word. How are we brought into touch with the revelation of the writers of Scripture?

6. To what does inspiration relate? State and refute some objections to this view.
7. State Dr. Pierson's comments on this view of inspiration.
8. What does Bishop Westcott affirm concerning the view of inspiration held by the Apostolic Church?
9. What is the outcome of this source, these instruments and these media?
10. In what ways is truth exhibited in the Bible?

10

INSPIRATION OF THE BIBLE
(Continued)

FORMER CONSIDERATIONS have shown that the Bible as a revelation of divine truth occupies a unique position, and that this uniqueness is due to some action of God whereby we are assured of the reality of the divine communication. This action is called Inspiration and in further study of it some important principles emerge.

1. *Varieties of Inspiration.* — It is of supreme importance to realize that Inspiration does not always mean the same thing, and for this reason it is essential to use the term with the greatest care and the strictest possible accuracy. Several vital and important distinctions must be made and kept in view.

(1) Sometimes Inspiration means a direct communication from God. When Paul said, "I have received from the Lord," he evidently claimed to have had a communication of truth direct from above. This corresponds exactly with the frequent claims made, as already seen, by prophets and others, when they said, "The Lord spake to me," etc. And such a direct revelation is obviously necessary, because many truths of the Bible are above and beyond human ken and must be revealed because they could not be discovered by man.

(2) Sometimes Inspiration means "the inspiration of selection." It is clear that the historical books of the Old Testament give mere fragments of the events out of the complete annals of the kingdoms of Israel and Judah, and in view of the emphasis indicated by the substance and arrangement of these books, a selection must have been made. In like manner, John selected materials out of our Lord's life to form the Fourth Gospel (John 20:31), and Luke's preface points in the same direction. Inspiration here is associated with the selection of materials.

(3) Sometimes Inspiration means only the guarantee of an accurate record. In the Bible we find the words of the Devil. They are not true, although they are found in the Bible. We find the words of Job's friends. They are not true, but they

INSPIRATION OF THE BIBLE

are in the Bible. We find the words of God's enemies in the Bible. They are not true. The sentiment is wrong, but the record of them is true. The sentiment may be full of imperfection, but the record is always perfect. This is the meaning of the inspiration of accurate record. We have to be very careful, therefore, that if a man preaches from a particular text, he first inquires who said it. An old Welsh preacher once gave out his text this way: "Skin for skin, yea, all that a man hath will he give for his life"; and then said, "That is a lie!" Of course it was. It is the word of Satan. Although it is in God's Book, it is not true of itself, but the record of it is true. There may be, there often is, imperfection in the sentiment, but there is no imperfection in the account of it.

This aspect of the subject calls attention to the distinction between Revelation and Inspiration. Revelation is the substance of God's truth, the *what*; Inspiration is the expression of that truth, the *how*. We can see this in 1 Corinthians 2: 10-13, where we have revelation in verse 10, and inspiration in verse 13. And so, not all the Bible is *revealed*, because much of it is history and refers to all sorts of men. But all in the Bible is *inspired*, because the record is given at every point in words that are trustworthy. This distinction helps us to understand how it is that the

Bible, while fully inspired, is not of the same spiritual value at every point. The revelation of truth is, as we have seen, progressive, but the record is accurate throughout.

2. *Inspiration and Difficulties.* — How is Inspiration to be regarded in the face of Bible difficulties? People often say the Bible is so difficult. It is. But when once we have decided, on the grounds of proper evidence, that the Bible is the Word of God, then every difficulty must be judged in the light of that antecedent fact. In the words of Tregelles, the great textual critic: "No difficulty in connection with a proved fact can invalidate the fact itself."

Some difficulties are inherent in a revelation, otherwise it would not be a revelation. We cannot expect that which comes from the infinite God to finite man to be without difficulty. Revelation means to "draw back the veil," and if there were no veil to draw back, we should not have any revelation. Therefore, we are not surprised if, as Butler taught us nearly two hundred years ago, there are difficulties in revelation, for there are difficulties in nature also, and yet nature is from the same God.

Difficulties are either scientific, historical, or ethical. Scientific difficulties for the most part turn upon differences of interpretation between man's views of the Bible and man's views of

INSPIRATION OF THE BIBLE

science. Difficulties of history have to be tested one by one; and we have yet to find any real statement in the Bible in terms of history that has been found to be unhistorical. And with regard to ethical difficulties, what has been said about progressive revelation may be applied at this point. God has revealed more and more of his will as man could bear it. There is, therefore, such a thing as progress in the ethics of the Bible, but there is no progress beyond the ethics of Christ and his apostles. Not a single new ethic has been given to the world since Jesus Christ and his apostles lived on this earth.

Then let us remember that none of these difficulties affect any fundamental Christian doctrine. Dean Farrar, who was no slave of conservatism, once said that no demonstrable error has ever been discovered in the Bible.

We are not called upon to answer every objection. It is quite sufficient for us to prove the truth of Christianity. Why should a man take leave of his common sense when he reads the Bible? There are scores of things in life that we cannot understand. A man says, "I will not believe what I do not see." Then what about his brains? So in regard to life. No one can tell us what life is. We cannot define life, and since we cannot, we ought not to be surprised if we find difficulties in the Bible that we cannot solve.

Let us make use of the Bible as fully as we can, and see how far that will take us. A man once went to Moody and said: "Mr. Moody, I cannot accept your Bible, because there are so many difficulties in it." Moody said to him: "Do you like fish?" "Yes." "Do you find any bones in it?" "Yes." "Do you eat them?" "No, I put them on the side of my plate." "That is what I do with the difficulties of the Bible, and I find quite enough fish without bones." That is a good, working, practical rule, though obviously it cannot settle everything. It is called the verifying faculty, and it is worth applying. It will do much to prove the uniqueness of the Bible.

3. *Inspiration and Criticism.*—There are three kinds of criticism, and these should be carefully kept together. The first is what is called Lower Criticism. This is the technical word descriptive of the criticism which provides a text and a translation. We depend upon scholarship for these. Since very few know Greek and Hebrew, we take our text from scholars, and also their translation. This is the lower or the lowest criticism, and is legitimate, important, and, of course, absolutely essential. And for all practical purposes either the Authorized or Revised Version does give us a substantial idea of the original text.

Then, secondly, there is what is called the

Higher Criticism. This has to do with the authorship, date, and character of the books; and again it is legitimate, vital, and essential, only it requires to be tested. Let us not call any man master, whether ancient or modern, English or German. Let us simply hold ourselves free to look at these things for ourselves. What is meant is that we must not merely follow a fashion of scholarship but test things for ourselves and get the theory that best fits all the facts.

But there is a third aspect, the "Highest" Criticism. It is sometimes overlooked. Here it is: "To this man will I look, even to him that is poor and of a contrite spirit and trembleth at my word" (Isa. 66:2). This is the criticism of the humble soul. To the same effect is another text: "The Word of God is a 'critic' of the thoughts and intents of the heart" (Heb. 4:12, Greek). If the soul of man will allow God's Word to criticize it, and if we do a little more "trembling" at God's Word, this will be the highest criticism, and will provide a criterion that would settle almost everything for us. The trouble is that people take the lower and the higher criticism, but forget the third, the highest. Yet, on the other hand, there are numbers of humble souls who know far more of the truth of Scripture than the greatest scholars. As James Hamilton once said: "A Christian on his knees sees farther than a philosopher on his tiptoes." When these three are held together there need be no fear about criticism. To appreciate the pictures on stained-glass windows we must go inside a church; and to know the Bible we must go inside, and not judge from the outside. Nor with reason only, but with conscience, and heart, and soul, and will; and when the whole nature responds to the highest criticism, rationalizing critical theories will not be able to do us any serious harm.

4. *Inspiration and Spiritual Work.*—Our view of Inspiration will depend very largely on the use we make of the Bible. If it is employed as a mere reference book our conception of it may be low, but if it is regarded as our daily food and the instrument of our Christian service, our view of it will be correspondingly high.

What does the Bible do for spiritual life and work? The Bible is spoken of as God's seed (Luke 8:11; Jas. 1:21). We are born of the Word (1 Pet. 1:23); we grow by the Word (1 Pet. 2:2); we are cleansed by the Word (John 15:3); we are sanctified by the Word (John 17:17); we are protected by the Word (Eph. 6:17); we are edified by the Word (Acts 20:32); we are illuminated by the Word (Psa. 119:105); we are converted by the Word (Psa. 19:11); and we are satisfied with the Word (Psa. 119:103). Surely a

INSPIRATION OF THE BIBLE

Word that can do all this must have divine power in it. There is a Latin phrase, *solvitur ambulando,* which is equivalent to our proverbial expression, "The proof of the pudding is in the eating." The Word of God in experience is the greatest proof we can have, and if we allow the things now mentioned to become part and parcel of our life, we shall know what the power of God's Word means.

Then from the work of the Bible in our own souls will come this verification of the Bible in our efforts on behalf of others. If we wish to verify the Bible, let us go out and win souls for Christ—do personal work. A great number of our problems are theoretical. They come from places where people spin theories absolutely remote from human life. But if we go out into the world and tell a man of the Lord Jesus Christ, and get that man to ask, "What must I do to be saved?" we shall very soon get verification of the Word of God; and when we have that, we shall not need much, if any, further testimony to its inspiration.

QUESTIONS

1. Does inspiration always mean the same thing? State and explain several varieties of inspiration found in the Word of God. Distinguish between inspiration and revelation.
2. Is all the Bible revealed? Why? Is all the Bible inspired? Why? What is the practical value of this distinction?

3. What was the dictum of Tregelles about difficulties? Are there difficulties in the Bible? Are these to be expected? Explain your answer in the light of the word "revelation."
4. How are the difficulties of the Bible to be classified? Out of what do scientific difficulties in the Bible generally arise?
5. How are historical difficulties to be handled? What proportion of historical statements in the Bible have been found to be defective? How are ethical difficulties to be explained?
6. Describe what is meant by the verifying faculty.
7. What kinds of criticism are there? In what field do the first two kinds labor?
8. What is meant by the "Highest Criticism"?
9. On what will our view of inspiration largely depend?
10. Name seven effects produced by the Word of God. How may we with certainty verify the claims of the Bible?

11

INTERPRETATION OF THE BIBLE

IT IS FREQUENTLY REMARKED that most of our difficulties with the Bible are connected with its interpretation. For example, instead of saying, as is so often done, that Science and the Bible disagree, it would be more correct to say that interpretations of Science and interpretations of the Bible disagree, since Science and the Bible, coming from the same divine source, cannot possibly be discordant. It is, therefore, of the first importance to give the most thorough consideration to certain principles which should guide us in our interpretation of Scripture.

1. In general the supreme need of the Holy Spirit must be emphasized. As the Bible is a

divine revelation it is essential that the readers should be in spiritual sympathy with its standpoint, accepting its authority and desiring to learn its meaning. An irreligious man cannot possibly obtain the true idea of Scripture or appreciate the standpoint of the writers. It is recorded of a well-known American Christian lady, Mrs. Margaret Bottome, that one Sunday afternoon she had been attending a Bible class in New York, and as she returned to her home she found a gentleman waiting for her, a professor in one of the colleges. When she expressed her regret at not having been at home on his arrival and explained that she had been attending the Bible class, a thinly veiled sneer came to her caller's face as he said: "Oh, you believe in the Bible, do you?" Her sensitive spirit at once felt the sneer and the plain inference from the words, and instantly she replied with a beautiful light on her face: "Oh, you know, I have the pleasure of a personal, intimate acquaintance with the Author of the Book!" It is impossible to exaggerate the importance of this spiritual standpoint in our approach to the Bible.

2. Then follows the necessity of studying the Book like other books, because the divine revelation has been given to us in book form. This will mean that we should give careful attention to matters of grammar, of history, and

INTERPRETATION OF THE BIBLE 107

of words, both in regard to their etymology and to their usage. In all this the obvious and natural meaning of the words and phrases should come first.

3. Yet, as we give attention to the Bible from beginning to end, we must always bear in mind its relation to Christ, for both Old and New Testaments are so closely associated with Him that he constitutes the key to the interpretation of many of its vital passages. In the Old Testament Christ is prepared for and anticipated in various ways, while in the New Testament he is seen to be manifested in Person, and the results of that manifestation are evident in the life and service of the Christian Church. It will be of real and constant value to keep in mind as we endeavor to interpret the Bible that its dominant note is "Christ in all the Scriptures."

4. And yet it is important to keep clear, what has already been emphasized in a former chapter, the progressiveness of the revelation of the Bible. This principle is the key which unlocks many of the difficulties, especially of the Old Testament.

5. In this connection it is also necessary to emphasize another point, which has already been considered, the differences of the dispensations which can be traced throughout Scripture. When we follow Augustine's advice to "distin-

guish the dispensations," many of our Bible problems find their solution.

6. Then, it is essential for us to distinguish rigidly between interpretation and application, between the primary and the secondary meanings of Scripture. It will probably be found necessary to apply this principle almost everywhere. To take one instance, perhaps the most familiar: In the Authorized Version the headings of the chapters from Isaiah 40 to 66 frequently refer to "the Church" as though the various messages found in that magnificent section had reference to the present dispensation, and to the body of Christ. But when the chapters are considered, it will be found that they have no reference to the Church at all, but to Israel, and this shows the vital necessity of the primary interpretation to Israel being distinguished from the secondary and spiritual application to the Church. The same principle obtains in the study of such passages as Isaiah 2:2 to 4 and Ezekiel 37. Whatever spiritual teaching we may derive from these passages for our life today, it is essential to keep in mind that the primary reference cannot possibly be to anything in the Gospel dispensation, but to something that is still future. As before stated—while all Scripture is written *for* us, it is not all written *to* us.

The New Testament affords almost constant

INTERPRETATION OF THE BIBLE 109

illustration of the same distinction. Thus, when we read Matthew 10:5 to 10 we see at once that the primary reference was purely local to the Jews, especially when we compare Luke 22:36. So also with Matthew 16:28. Further, the reference to Joel, chapter 2, by the apostle Peter on the Day of Pentecost (Acts 2) is a striking illustration of this principle, for it is obvious that the prophecy of Joel was not by any means completely fulfilled in what happened then. See also the reference to John the Baptist in Malachi 4:5. While it is, of course, true as our Lord said, that the Baptist in relation to Christ was "Elijah the prophet" (Matt. 11:14), yet the text speaks of "a great and terrible day of the Lord," which shows that there is a further and fuller realization to come. Another illustration out of many is afforded by the familiar words of the Lord's Prayer. When Christ taught his disciples to pray to their Father in heaven, "Thy Kingdom come," it seems clear that he was referring to a time beyond the mediatorial Kingdom of the Son, even to the end of all things, when the Son shall have delivered up the Kingdom to the Father (1 Cor. 15:24).

7. Another vital principle of interpretation is the need of distinguishing rigidly between the literal and symbolical views of passages. The Bible is an Eastern Book and as such it is full of

pictures and metaphors. We must take the literal meaning whenever it is possible. One instance of this is in Luke 1:31-33, where eight statements are made concerning our Lord. As the first five of these are literally fulfilled in the first coming of Christ, it seems impossible to doubt that the other three are to be literally fulfilled when he comes again, for it is not natural to take the former literally and then to spiritualize the latter. On the other hand, there are many obvious instances of the purely symbolical meaning, so illustrative of Eastern life. Thus, in Psalm 68:16, the mountains are said to leap. In the book of Revelation we have an almost constant use of metaphor and symbol, like the "sea of glass" and many other instances. The use of allegory is found in Scripture, as in Galatians 4:22-31, though, as we know, this was based on the historical circumstances of Hagar and Ishmael. It will, no doubt, be difficult from time to time to express the distinction between what is literal and what is symbolical, and yet it is essential that the attempt be made.

8. Closely associated with the foregoing is the frequent use of figurative language in Scripture, and it is important to remember that this form of speech intensifies a fact and does not destroy it. It means, as we know, that one thing is put for another. Among the very many illustrations of

this, which is peculiarly characteristic of Eastern life, may be adduced the following: "My cup runneth over" (Psa. 23:5); "My grey hairs with sorrow" (Gen. 42:38). There is also the particular form of figurative language known as personification, as "The blood that speaketh" (Heb. 12:24); "Let not thy left hand know—" (Matt. 6:3). The use of exaggeration is found in the well-known phrase, "hateth not . . . he cannot be my disciple" (Luke 14:26). Then, there are metaphors and parables in almost every part of the Scripture.

But the most important feature of the figurative language found in Scripture is known as type, which has long been described as "an illustration in a lower sphere of a truth belonging to a higher." A type is a pictorial or personal representation of something that is to come, and the following distinctions have been drawn. A parable is an illustration in word, while a type is an illustration in deed. A prophecy is a prediction, while a type is an anticipation. An allegory is an illustration in the form of fancy, while a type is one in the form of fact. A symbol is an illustration which gives a hint, merely suggesting a truth, while a type is an illustration which is fuller and provides a completer view. It is also said that a parable illustrates a truth that concerns the present, while a type deals with that which is still future, the object of the type being to prepare the mind for the true idea of the coming redemption.

The following principles have been set forth for the proper interpretation of the types. (1) Each type suggests some great truth, though the resemblance is internal rather than external. (2) Each type is necessarily imperfect in the conveyance of the truth. (3) The New Testament is our best guide to the meaning of types. Beyond this it is essential to take great care, lest we regard as typical what was not intended by God so to be.

9. Not least of all in importance is the absolute necessity of studying the context when we are concerned with any particular passage. It is well known that theological students are often advised when they take a text to "study the context, lest the text become a pretext." Out of the many illustrations which show the necessity of this principle, the chapter divisions of the Authorized Version may be adduced. Thus, if we read John 3:1, only, it is probably difficult, if not impossible, to see precisely what sort of a man Nicodemus was, but if that verse is considered strictly in connection with the three preceding verses, and the particle in the Greek, which has been curiously omitted from the Authorized Version, be borne in mind, it is not difficult to

understand the man's true character at that time. So, when the little word "also" in Luke 16:1 is carefully noted, it will be seen that the parable of the unjust steward is an application to the disciples of what our Lord had said to the Pharisees. He had been blamed for making friends of the poor and outcast (Luke 15:1, 2), but he vindicated himself, in the three parables of the lost sheep, the lost silver, and the lost son, and then applied the lesson to his own disciples and urged them to make to themselves friends of these poor people. Other illustrations of this vital principle can be found almost everywhere, but perhaps the most familiar, as it is in some respects the most important for many, is the statement of our Lord at the institution of the Last Supper. The words, "This is my body," are often quoted in certain quarters, and yet Christ said more than this, for He did not speak of the bread but of his sacrifice on the Cross: "This is my body which is being given for you" (1 Cor. 11:24).

These are not the only points to be remembered in connection with the interpretation of Scripture, but they will suffice to show how important it is to give careful attention to the circumstances of the Book, its Eastern origin, its spiritual meaning, and its practical message for daily life.

QUESTIONS

1. What is the source of most of the difficulties of the Bible? Is it correct to say, "Science and the Bible disagree"? What would be a truer way of expressing it?
2. What is the supreme need to be emphasized in the study of the Bible? Why?
3. How should the Bible be studied? Explain fully. What key is given for the interpretation of the Bible?
4. What bearing has progressiveness of revelation on the interpretation of the Bible?
5. Distinguish between interpretation and application. Give two illustrations of what is meant by this.
6. Between what two views of a passage must there always be careful distinction? What rule may be safely followed? Illustrate.
7. How is figurative language to be interpreted? What is the force of a figure of speech? What is a figure of speech? Give three illustrations.
8. What is the most important example of figurative language? Define this.
9. What principles have been given for the interpretation of types?
10. What important rule is to be followed in all study of the Bible?

12

PURPOSE OF THE BIBLE

OUR CONSIDERATION of the various aspects of Scripture naturally leads to the inquiry as to the aim and object of our use of the Bible, because everything else necessarily culminates in the definite relation of the Word of God to our own life. Since God has spoken, it is for us to hear and heed, and this will mean a proper use of Scripture.

1. *Its Stages.* — The first stage of all study in relation to the Bible is that known as Textual Criticism — the discovery of the true text, the assurance that we have as nearly as is possible for us to obtain them the words of the sacred writers. But this stage of study is obviously only

introductory. It is essential as the foundation, but is only the foundation.

The next stage is that which is known as Literary Criticism — the study of the Bible as literature, the consideration of its composition, authorship, date, style, and contents. This also is important and essential, for without it we should lose much of the beauty and glory of the Bible. Yet there is something more and better to which we must proceed. The Bible is literature, but it is more, and if we rest content at this stage we shall fail at a vital point.

The third stage of Bible study is concerned with Biblical Exegesis — that is, the true interpretation of the contents of the Bible, the exact meaning of passages, sections, and verses. This involves a knowledge of language and grammar, of manners and customs, of literary and rhetorical forms of expression. This is obviously of the greatest moment and imperative for all true study. Still, it is not everything, and it is only too possible to become occupied with details of interpretation, and all the while to be missing the essential spiritual power.

The fourth stage of our work with the Bible is occupied with Biblical Theology—the consideration of the religion revealed in the Scriptures, its doctrines, morals and duties. This is the highest point of Christian scholarship, and it is of the utmost value to be able to see what is the theological teaching of each stage of God's revelation of Himself, from the first days until the time of our Lord Jesus Christ. Yet even here we do not get finality; for it is only too possible to be occupied with the intellectual contents of the Bible, to have it all arranged and grasped in our minds, and still to be devoid of the substance and power of the Word of God.

Through and above all stages we must press until we arrive at the summit, which is the use of the Bible as God's personal Word to our own souls, "What saith my Lord unto his servant?" "What wilt Thou have me to do?" The Scriptures are intended to lead the soul direct to God, to introduce it to His presence, and to convey His revelation of truth and grace. If we do not realize this, we shall fail at the critical point, and all our other knowledge, great and valuable though it be, will count for little or nothing. Bible study above all else is intended to bring and keep the soul in direct contact with God. The highest privilege and holiest possibility of the Christian religion is fellowship with God in Christ, and this is absolutely impracticable apart from constant devotional dealings with the Word of God.

2. *Its Requirements.* — Any one with intellect can become an expert in the first four stages of

the Bible study referred to above. The fifth stage needs qualities and conditions far beyond intellectual capacity and attainment.

The soul must be accepted with God in Christ. Fellowship with God is only possible to a saved soul, to one pardoned and accepted in Christ. Sin must be dealt with before communion is realized, and consequently there can be no genuine devotional study of Scripture apart from the position of a believer in Christ and the assurance of personal salvation. The "natural" man receiveth not the things of the Spirit of God, or, to take Paul's word literally, "does not welcome" them. But, more than this, as the apostle goes on to say, "neither is he able to experience them" (1 Cor. 2:14, Greek); he has not the faculty which will enable him to do so. He must be changed into a "spiritual" man, for these things are "spiritually discerned." It is for lack of realization of this patent and potent fact that so much error is abroad today. Men study the Bible without being at all conscious that it demands spiritual as well as intellectual qualifications.

Further, the soul thus accepted in Christ must be kept right with God, if Bible study is to be of the highest and best. The life of the believer must be true to God. The conscience must be kept pure and sensitive; the mind must be kept teachable,

Purpose of the Bible

self-distrustful, and ever wishful to learn more; the will must be kept submissive and obedient, and ready to do what God appoints. The secrets of the Lord are only revealed to "them that fear Him"; for "to this man will I look, even to him that ... trembleth at my Word." Many a believer finds the Word of God dark to him because he is out of spiritual condition. There is no "open vision" because his soul is not right with God. The devotional study of the Bible is at once a cause and an effect in relation to the spiritual life. It is a cause of increased spiritual vitality, power, insight and blessing, while in turn this spiritual reality of life leads to yet more spiritual revelation of God in His Word. Prayer and Obedience are organs of knowledge, and the more of these the more knowledge. For spiritual power in life we must use the spiritual food of the Word of God.

3. *Its Methods.* — For the devotional and spiritual use of the Word of God there are three rules, but these three, though simple, are all-inclusive.

We must *search* (John 5:39). God's thoughts are never revealed to listless readers, only to eager searchers. The glories of the Scriptures are not to be discovered without diligent search. The Bible is like a mine, and its jewels are not to be picked up on the roadside. It affords opportunity for thought, and requires its exercise. Its words, phrases and sentences are full of meaning and power. Like our Lord's parables, the Bible at once conceals and reveals its message. Strenuous thought is imperative if we would obtain from the Word the blessing it contains. We must ponder its statements, dwell on its meaning, grasp its message, and dwell lovingly and earnestly on its revelation of God in Christ. Nothing in it is without some purpose, and what this is, the Lord will reveal in response to His servants' faithful search.

We must *meditate* (Josh. 1:8; Psa. 1:2). "Meditation" comes from a Greek word meaning "to attend," and this is essentially the idea of the Bible meditation. It is reading with attention. More than this, it is reading with *intention*. It is concerned at each point with personal application. And it must be our own thought, our own musing, our own application. The great, the primary, the essential point is *first-hand* meditation on God's Word as the secret of Christian living.

Dr. Andrew Murray has reminded us in one of his books that milk represents food which has already passed through digestive processes before it is taken by us. So we may say that all the little books of devotion, the helps to holiness, the series of manuals of thought and teaching, however valuable, represent food which has passed through the spiritual digestion of others before it comes to us. And it should be used as such. If these helps are put first, to the exclusion of the Bible alone, and the Bible day by day, they will become dangerous and disastrous, crutches that prevent vigorous exercise, and lead to spiritual senility. If they are put second, they become delightful and valuable, inspirations to further thought and pathways to deeper blessings. When we have had our own meditation of the Word, we are the better able to enjoy what God teaches us through others of his children, and especially those whom God honors with special gifts of teaching.

Mediation must be real. It must be "the meditation of my heart" (Psa. 49:3), and "the heart" in Scripture means the center of the moral being, which includes the intellect, emotions, and the will. It implies that we come to the Word to be searched thoroughly, guided definitely, and strengthened effectually. The hour of meditation is not a time for dreamy, vague imaginings, but for living, actual blessing, whether in the form of guidance, warning, comfort, or counsel.

Mediation will also be practical. What are its stages or elements? First, the careful reading of the particular passage or subject, thinking over its real and original meaning. Next, a resolute application of it to my own life's needs, conscience, heart, mind, imagination, will; finding out what it has to say to me. Next, a hearty turning of it into prayer for mercy and grace, that its teaching may become part of my life. Next, a sincere transfusion of it into resolution that my life shall reproduce it. Lastly, a whole-hearted surrender to, and trust in, God for power to practise it forthwith and constantly throughout the day.

We must *compare* (1 Cor. 2:13). God's Word is like a kaleidoscope with many combinations. In addition to our search and meditation of one particular passage, we must compare passages together, in order to arrive at the full meaning of the Word which has been given to us in "many parts and many manners" (Heb. 1:1). The various aspects of truth are thus seen in their entirety and proportion, and our spiritual life becomes fully informed and completely equipped. There are so many topics or subjects scattered throughout God's Word, that only as we collect and compare them can we appreciate the fulness and glory of God's revelation.

All that has been said may be summed up in the words of Job: "I have esteemed the words of his mouth more than my necessary food"; and of Jeremiah: "Thy words were found and I did eat them"; and of the Psalmist: "How sweet are thy words to my taste!" The Bible must be our daily

Purpose of the Bible

food if we are to be strong and vigorous. Not quantity, but quality, determines the nutritive value of food. What we must emphasize is capacity to receive, power to assimilate, and readiness to reproduce. As some one has well put it, the process is threefold—infusion, suffusion, transfusion.

The Word thus becomes all-sufficient and all-powerful in our life—the mirror to reveal (Jas. 1); the water to cleanse (Eph. 5); the milk to nourish (1 Pet. 2); the strong meat to invigorate (Heb. 5); the honey to delight (Psa. 119); the fire to warm (Jer. 23); the hammer to break and fasten (Jer. 23); the sword to fight (Eph. 6); the seed to grow (Matt. 13); the lamp to guide (Psa 119); the statute-book to legislate (Psa. 119); and the gold to treasure in time and for eternity (Psa. 19).

QUESTIONS

1. Name and describe fully the first two stages of the study of the Bible.
2. Name and describe fully the next two stages of the study of the Bible.
3. Describe fully the highest stage of study.
4. What requirements are necessary for proficiency in the first four stages?
5. Describe fully two requirements for proficiency in the fifth stage.
6. How many essential rules are there for the devotional and spiritual use of the Scriptures? Explain fully the first of them.

7. What is the second rule? Discuss it in its several aspects.
8. What is the third rule? Discuss it fully.
9. How may all that has been said be summarized?
10. What does the Word of God thus become?